PERIODS

EVERYTHING YOU NEED TO KNOW

Published in the UK by Scholastic, 2026
Scholastic, Bosworth Avenue, Warwick, CV34 6UQ
Scholastic Ireland, 89E Lagan Road, Dublin Industrial Estate, Glasnevin, Dublin, D11 HP5F

SCHOLASTIC and associated logos are trademarks and/or
registered trademarks of Scholastic Inc.

Text © Dr Emily MacDonagh, 2026
Inside illustrations © Jasmine Parker, 2026
Cover photo by Anita Kot/Moment via Getty Images

Written in collaboration with Consultant Paediatrician Dr Rebecca Mann.

The moral rights of the author and illustrator have been asserted by them.

ISBN 978 0702 32353 9

A CIP catalogue record for this book is available from the British Library.

Printed and bound in Great Britain by Bell and Bain Ltd, Glasgow
Paper made from wood grown in sustainable forests and other controlled sources.

MIX
Paper | Supporting
responsible forestry
FSC
www.fsc.org
FSC® C007785

1 3 5 7 9 10 8 6 4 2

www.scholastic.co.uk

For safety or quality concerns:
UK: www.scholastic.co.uk/productinformation
EU: www.scholastic.ie/productinformation

CONTENTS

WELCOME TO THE JOURNEY

Hi there! So, you've either just started your periods or you're waiting for them to arrive and are feeling a little confused, curious or maybe even a bit worried. Or maybe you've had your period for a while, and just want to learn more about it. Whichever it is, you're in the right place.

Welcome to a book that's all about periods... written by a doctor (that's me – **Dr Emily!**) who's not just here to throw a bunch of medical facts at you, but to talk **honestly**, **practically** and openly about WHAT'S REALLY GOING ON.

Let's be honest: getting your period is a **big deal**. It's one of the major milestones of growing up, and it means your body is doing something pretty amazing – changing from a girl into a woman, and getting ready to **(if you choose to)** have a baby one day. But before we get there **(no rush!)**, there's a lot to learn, and that's where this book comes in.

We'll cover the **science-y stuff**, of course – what's happening in your body, how **hormones** play a part, and what's considered **'normal'**. But more importantly, we'll also talk about the stuff that *really* matters day to day: how to manage your period, how to deal with the ups and downs, what products you can use, how to talk to people about it, and how to know when something's not quite right.

This book is here to be your PERIOD PAL. Think of it as a reassuring guide that helps you feel more **confident**, **calm** and **in control**, no matter where you are on your period journey. By the end, you'll be able to understand your body, know what works best for you, and feel totally okay asking for help when you need it.

Because your period is nothing to fear, it's just part of what makes you, *you*.

LET'S GET STARTED!

UNDERSTANDING YOUR CHANGING BODY

This first section is all about **puberty**, the changes you might be experiencing, and your **first period**. If you're at the beginning of your period journey, you might find it helpful to start with this section, however if you're more experienced and want to skip ahead to **The Science of Periods** on page 10 or **Tracking and Understanding Your Cycle** on page 54, feel free!

WHAT'S THE DEAL WITH PUBERTY AND PERIODS?

If you want to understand what's happening when you start your period, it helps to first understand **puberty**.

Puberty is your body's way of getting you ready to grow into an **adult**. That means **growing taller**, **changing shape**, and **getting things working in a different way inside your body**.

But puberty isn't just about physical stuff. Your brain and emotions are changing too. You'll probably start **thinking differently**, **feeling new emotions** and **becoming more independent**. You might also become interested in new things or in building different kinds of friendships.

SO, WHAT ACTUALLY IS PUBERTY?

Puberty is the name for all the **changes** your body and mind go through as you grow from a child into an adult. Everyone goes through it, but not always at the same time or in the same way. Here are a few terms that are handy to know:

Acne – spots that appear on your face, back or chest because of hormones.

Boobs (breasts) – the front of your chest that grows during puberty. Your nipples will get bigger too.

Emotions – feelings like happiness, anger or sadness. These can intensify during puberty!

Genitals – your private parts. This term is mainly used for the parts that are visible from the outside – which include the labia (the folds of skin around your vagina) and the entrance to the vagina.

Reproductive organs – the more complicated parts are inside your body and include the vagina, uterus and ovaries (see page 11 to find out what these are).

Hormones – chemicals that tell your body how and when to grow or change.

Ovaries – organs that store and release eggs.

Period – the blood that comes out of your vagina each month. It means your body is becoming capable of pregnancy.

Pituitary gland – a tiny gland in your brain that acts like the 'organizer' of puberty. It sends out the chemical messengers (hormones) that help move your body through the changes it needs as you go through puberty.

Puberty – the process of growing into a teen and eventually an adult.

Pubic hair – hair that grows around your genital area.

Vagina – a stretchy tube inside your body that connects the outside genitals to your uterus. Blood comes out through it during your period. It is the passageway a baby comes through when it is born during a vaginal birth.

THE BRAIN'S IN CHARGE

Your brain kicks off puberty by sending out signals using chemical messengers called **hormones**. It starts when the brain tells your ovaries to make a hormone called **oestrogen**, which triggers all kinds of changes.

Another hormone, **testosterone** (yep, girls have it too!), helps with growing body hair and makes you grow faster.

Here's what puberty might look like for girls:

- Your breasts start to grow
- You grow taller
- Your hips get wider
- You might put on weight in new areas like your thighs or upper arms
- Hair starts growing under your arms, on your legs and around your genitals
- You sweat more easily
- You might get spots
- You'll feel new emotions
- And eventually ... you'll start your periods

It might sound like a lot, but don't panic, these changes happen slowly, over a few years. You're not going to wake up tomorrow with a completely different body.

Let's talk a bit more about those changes...

BOOBS, GROWTH SPURTS AND BODY SHAPE

Breasts start growing with something called **'BREAST BUDS'**, which are small, hard lumps under your nipples. They might feel **sore** or **achy** at first, especially when touched or if you're moving around a lot. Don't worry, that's totally normal. Over time, they'll become softer and rounder.

During puberty, you can grow up to **10 cm** a year, much faster than when you were younger. Most of this growing happens when you're **asleep**, which is why teenagers often need more sleep than kids or adults.

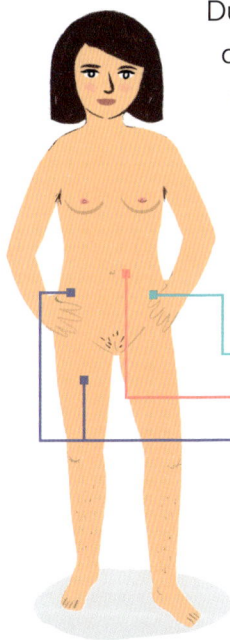

Your body shape also changes:
YOUR HIPS WIDEN
YOUR WAIST MAY APPEAR NARROWER
YOUR BODY STARTS STORING FAT IN DIFFERENT PLACES LIKE YOUR THIGHS AND HIPS

HAIR, SWEAT AND ALL THAT STUFF

BODY HAIR starts to grow under your arms and around your pubic area. It is darker and thicker than the rest of your body hair – this is completely normal.

You'll also **sweat more**, especially from your armpits. That's your body's way of cooling down. It's a good time to start wearing deodorant and maybe showering more often. The odour from armpits includes chemicals called **pheromones** that are said to cause a chemical reaction in the people around us. But if you sweat a lot and the sweat becomes stale, it can smell less than attractive! So in general, people wear an antiperspirant (to reduce the amount of sweat) and a deodorant (to remove less pleasant smells), particularly in warm weather or if they are going to be exercising.

WHAT'S HAPPENING 'DOWN THERE'?

OESTROGEN causes changes in your genital area too. You might notice that your **labia** (folds of skin around your vagina) and **clitoris** get bigger. Everyone's private parts look different, and that's totally normal – **there's no one 'right' way for them to look.**

You'll also start getting a white or clear liquid in your underwear – this is a small amount of mucus, often called a **'DISCHARGE'**. It's just your body's way of keeping things clean and healthy. You don't need to do anything unless it starts to smell unpleasant or look unusual – if that happens, you can talk to your doctor. Otherwise, just shower regularly and change your underwear every day.

Now, before we finally get to talk about periods, do remember that puberty can be a complicated time, **emotionally** and **physically**, and you don't have to go through it alone. Talk to someone you trust if you ever feel confused, embarrassed or worried. Everyone goes through this, and every body is different.

Once your body's been doing all of this changing for a while, your periods will usually start. And that brings us to the topic we are here to read about!

SO
LET'S GET
INTO IT...

THE SCIENCE
OF PERIODS

Now **science** isn't for everyone, but I really like to understand how the body works and why things happen. So if that interests you, then read on! If not, you can skip to the next section.

Before we get into exactly what periods are and the science behind them, let's take a look at the parts of your body involved in having a period – called the **'female reproductive system'**. We mentioned some of these parts on page 5, but check out the diagram for a bit more information...

FALLOPIAN TUBES

UTERUS

FIMBRIAE

OVARY

OVARY

ENDOMETRIUM

VAGINA

CERVIX

OVARY

EGG

UTERUS

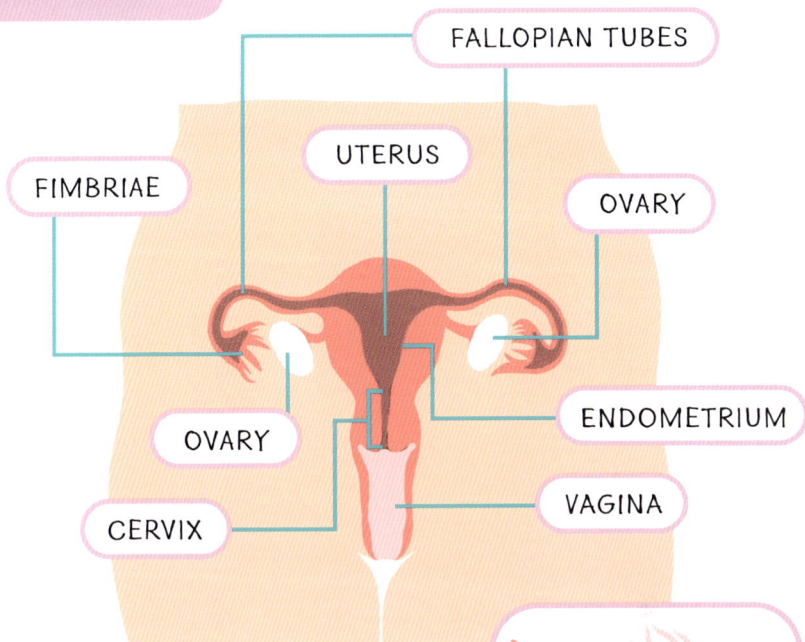

OVARIES: you have **two ovaries**. They are organs that store and then release eggs near the fimbriae which wafts them into the fallopian tube. Girls are actually born with **all the eggs** they will produce already present in the ovaries. In fact, all these eggs already exist inside a baby girl while she is still inside her mother's womb!

FIMBRIAE: these are like tiny fingers near to each ovary. They help move the egg from the ovary into the fallopian tube.

FALLOPIAN TUBES: you also have two of these, one leading from each ovary to either side of your uterus.

UTERUS: you may have heard of the word **'womb'** – this is just another word for the uterus. It is like an upside down pear-shaped structure found deep in the pelvis. The walls, which are **soft** and **muscular**, can stretch much bigger to hold a growing baby when someone is pregnant.

ENDOMETRIUM: the soft tissue lining the inside of the uterus. It grows **thicker** in preparation for a baby to grow within the uterus.

CERVIX: the cervix is right at the bottom of the uterus and connects it to the vagina.

VAGINA: the vagina is a stretchy tube inside your body that connects to your uterus. Blood comes out through it during your period. It is the way out of the uterus for a baby when it is delivered by a vaginal birth.

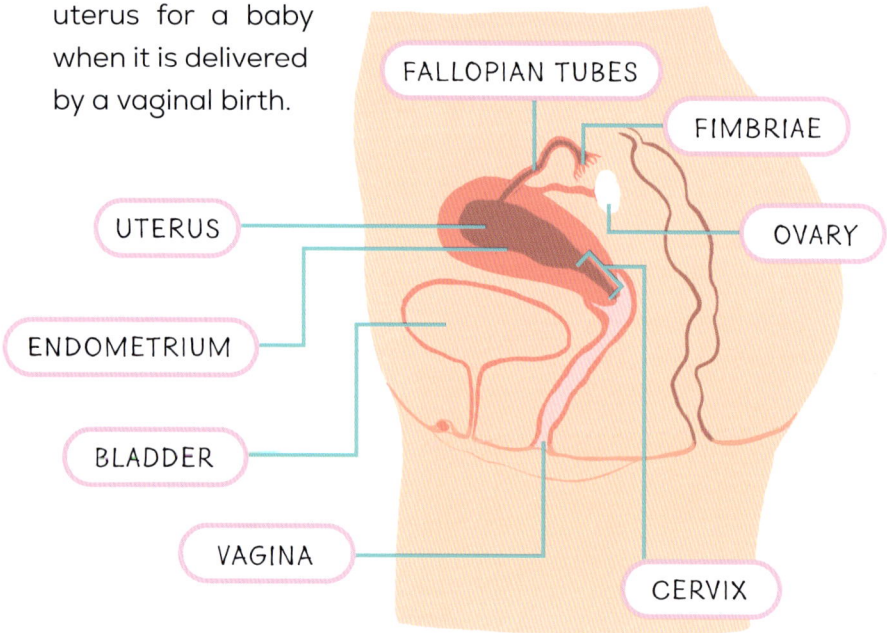

SIDE VIEW

FALLOPIAN TUBES

FIMBRIAE

UTERUS

OVARY

ENDOMETRIUM

BLADDER

VAGINA

CERVIX

SO WHERE DO YOU WEE FROM? When you have a wee, urine comes from the **bladder** down a completely separate tube **(called the urethra)**. The urethral opening sits in front of the vagina – but you can't easily see the opening because it is so small.

SO, WHAT EXACTLY IS A PERIOD?

Having periods is a natural part of life for anyone with a uterus and ovaries. During puberty, your body starts releasing an egg about once a month. That egg travels from the ovary to the uterus. Meanwhile, the lining of your uterus **(also called the endometrium)** thickens – just in case the egg gets fertilized by sperm and starts to grow into a baby. If that *doesn't* happen, the egg and the lining aren't needed anymore, so your body gets rid of them. That's what a period is – the lining and egg leaving your body through your vagina. You'll usually bleed for a few days each month.

Everyone's period is different. Some people bleed more **(that's called a 'heavy' period)** and some bleed less **(a 'light' period)**. It can *feel* like you're losing a lot of blood, but most people only lose about **6 to 8 teaspoons** during a whole period – some a bit more, some a bit less. Over time, you'll figure out what's normal for you and how to manage it. On page 105 you can read more about what might cause a person to have heavier (or lighter) periods, and what you can do if you are worried about it.

Sometimes, a person releases more than one egg in a month. This happens more often when you're younger **(like in your late teens)** or older **(early 40s)**. That's actually one reason why twins are more likely if someone has a baby really young or later in life.

QUICK STAT:
One in 65 pregnancies is a twin pregnancy, and **1 in 5,000 pregnancies results in triplets**. That's a lot of nappies! If you have released two separate eggs that get fertilized by two separate sperms, you will have **'non identical'** twins. Even less often, the woman produces a single egg that is fertilized and then later splits into two. This is how **'identical'** twins are formed. The babies will look almost exactly the same because they come from the same egg, so they have the same genes.

Let's delve a little more into the science behind periods. **Where exactly does the egg come from, and where does it go after it has been released?**

THE JOURNEY OF AN EGG...

The diagram on page 15 explains a little bit about the journey that an egg will make, from your ovaries where it is produced until it leaves your body through the vagina. Let's have a closer look at the steps:

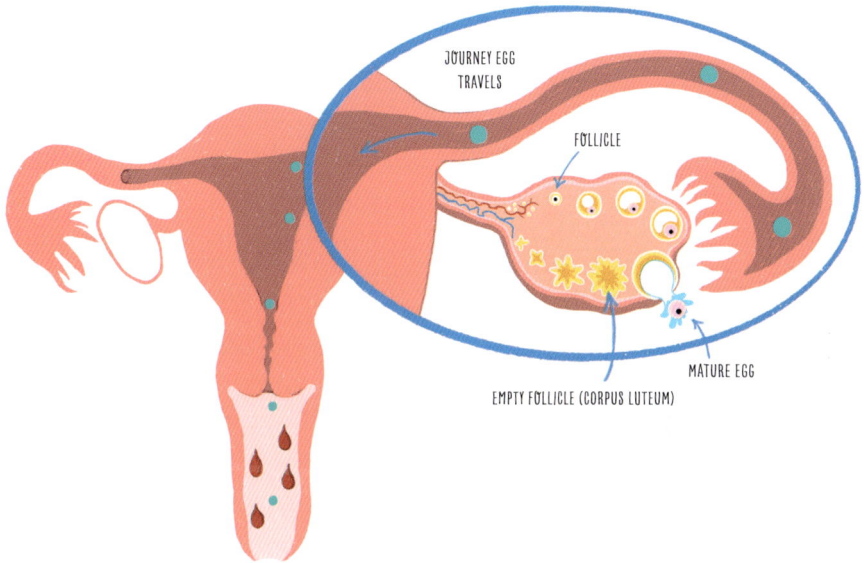

JOURNEY EGG TRAVELS

FOLLICLE

MATURE EGG

EMPTY FOLLICLE (CORPUS LUTEUM)

1. Remember how we said earlier that you are born with all the eggs you will need for your whole life in your ovaries? Well, each month, several of these eggs will start to mature inside the ovary. They begin to develop into small sacs called **follicles**.

2. One of these follicles will develop faster than the rest and become dominant, as the egg inside it begins to mature – in other words, one egg will get ready to be released from the ovary.

3 When the egg is ready, a surge of hormones will cause it to be released from the follicle. This is called **ovulation**. It is then captured by the fimbriae – remember these are tiny fingers near to the ovary that catch the egg and guide it into the **fallopian tube**.

4 Around this time, the **endometrium** (lining of the uterus) also starts to thicken to get ready to receive a fertilized egg (an egg that has met a sperm and could develop into a baby).

5 The egg travels down the fallopian tube towards the **uterus**. It is at this stage, if sperm were to be present, that the egg would usually be fertilized.

6 The egg continues its journey to the uterus.

7 If the egg is not fertilized, it does not stay in the uterus. Instead, it leaves your body through the vagina, along with the lining of the endometrium. In most girls and women, for most months of their life, the egg is not fertilized and they will have a period as the egg and uterine lining are released.

CLEVER CHEMICALS

Now, you might be wondering – how do the ovaries know to release an egg every month? And what makes the endometrium thicken at exactly the right time? Well, it all comes down to **hormones**. On page 6 we talked about hormones, how they are like tiny chemical messengers that are in charge of puberty and all the changes you will see and feel in your body. Periods are no different. There are quite a few different hormones that control your periods, so let's read more about them.

UNDERSTANDING OVULATION AND YOUR MONTHLY PERIOD: HOW HORMONES WORK IN THE MENSTRUAL CYCLE

Although the bit of your period that you see **(when you have some bleeding)** usually only lasts for a few days each month, there is a lot more going on in your body before and after this happens. The proper name for this is the **'menstrual cycle'**. That is why one of the medical terms for having your periods is **'menstruation'**. The menstrual cycle is controlled by hormones and usually lasts around **28 days**, although it can be a bit shorter or longer in different people. Two of the main things that happen during the menstrual cycle are the releasing of an egg **(ovulation)** and having a period **(menstrual bleeding)**. Let's break down what these things are, how they're connected, and why they happen – especially in terms of hormones.

WHAT IS THE MENSTRUAL CYCLE?

The menstrual cycle is the process your body goes through to prepare for a possible pregnancy each month. It involves your **brain**, **ovaries**, **uterus** and **hormones** working together. This monthly cycle is counted as starting from the first day of your period. So, for example, an **'average'** cycle will begin on day 1 (the first day of bleeding), you will release an egg from the ovary on day 14, and then the egg and the lining of the uterus will be almost ready to pass out of your body on day 28. **Then the cycle starts again!**

THE ROLE OF HORMONES

In the menstrual cycle, four important hormones are involved. They have quite complicated names, but I guess they do a pretty complicated job!

- **FSH (follicle-stimulating hormone)**
- **LH (luteinizing hormone)**
- **OESTROGEN**
- **PROGESTERONE**

Let's quickly take a look at each hormone in more detail before learning more about how they control the menstrual cycle.

FSH

FOLLICLE GROWTH

OESTROGEN

FSH is made by the pituitary gland in the brain. It starts to make the follicles grow in the ovaries, and also tells the ovaries to make oestrogen.

LH

LH is also produced by the pituitary gland. A surge of LH is what triggers ovulation (the release of an egg from the ovary).

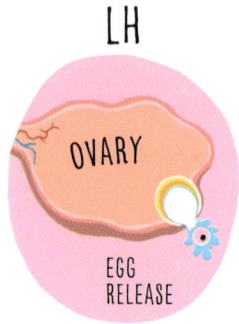

OVARY

EGG
RELEASE

OESTROGEN

FSH

THICKENS
UTERUS

LH

Oestrogen is made by the ovaries. It has a few jobs, including thickening the lining of the uterus. It also causes the pituitary to release LH and stops it releasing more FSH.

Progesterone is made by the leftover/empty follicle in the ovary after the egg has been released. It keeps the endometrium thick so it is ready for a fertilized egg.

PROGESTERONE

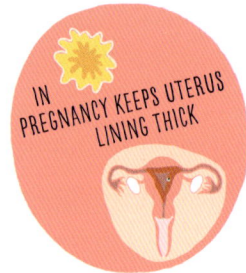

IN
PREGNANCY KEEPS UTERUS
LINING THICK

These hormones work together like a team, rising and falling at different times during the cycle. This causes the changes in the ovaries and uterus. Each phase might last slightly longer or be slightly shorter in different people, but below is a rough guide to the timings and how it all works.

THERE ARE FOUR MAIN PHASES IN THE CYCLE:

1. MENSTRUAL PHASE (when you are bleeding)
2. FOLLICULAR PHASE (before you ovulate)
3. OVULATION (release of the egg)
4. LUTEAL PHASE (after ovulation and before your next bleed)

Now, let's walk through each phase and see how the hormones are involved.

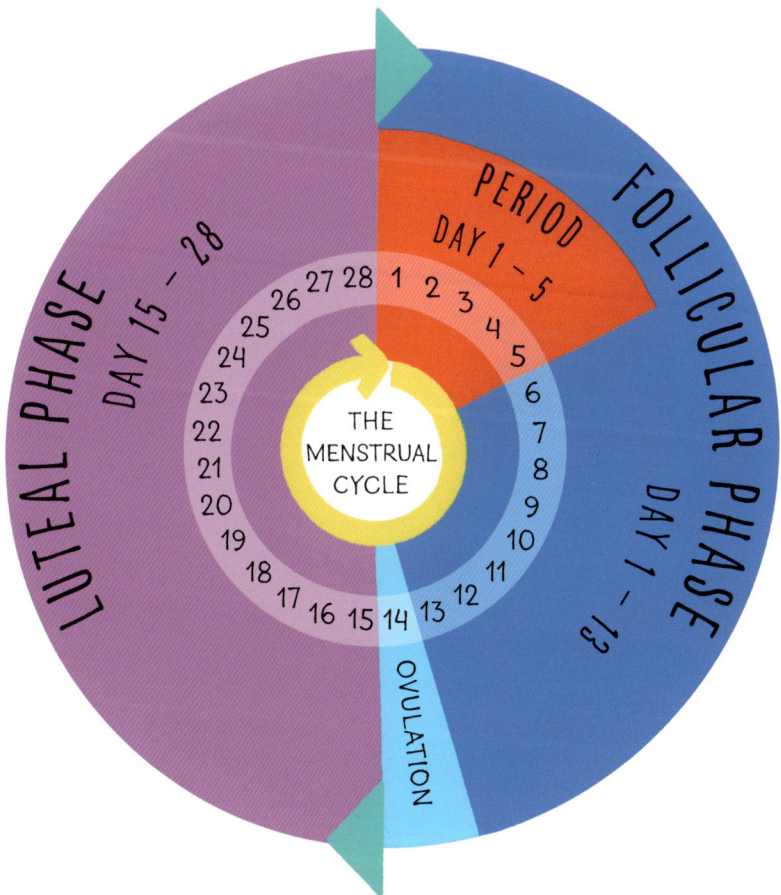

THE MENSTRUAL CYCLE

PERIOD DAY 1 – 5

FOLLICULAR PHASE DAY 1 – 13

OVULATION

LUTEAL PHASE DAY 15 – 28

28 1 2 3 4 5 6 7 8 9 10 11 12 13 14 15 16 17 18 19 20 21 22 23 24 25 26 27

PHASE 1: Menstrual Phase (day 1–5)

This is when your period **(bleeding)** happens. Most people think of day 1 of their cycle as being the first day they start bleeding, then you count your monthly cycle from there. The egg from the previous month's cycle leaves the uterus when the body realizes it's **not** pregnant. Since there's no pregnancy, hormone levels – especially **oestrogen** and **progesterone** – drop. This causes the lining of the uterus **(the endometrium)**, which had built up during the previous cycle, to break down and leave the body through the vagina.

At the same time, the brain starts releasing more **FSH** to begin preparing for the next cycle.

PHASE 2: Follicular Phase (day 1–13)

Even though this phase technically starts at the same time as your period, it continues after the bleeding stops, so we call this the second phase. During this phase, the hormone **FSH** helps your ovaries develop several tiny sacs called **follicles**. Each follicle contains an **egg**, but usually only one will become the **'dominant'** one – the one that will fully mature and be released. FSH stands for **'follicle stimulating hormone'** – and that is exactly what it does! – the brain releases **FSH** to stimulate the ovary to produce a follicle so an egg can be released.

As the follicles grow, they release oestrogen. Oestrogen helps build the uterine lining so it is ready to receive the egg – just in case it is fertilized and a pregnancy happens.

PHASE 3: Ovulation (around day 14)

When enough oestrogen has been released by the follicles, the brain responds by releasing a sudden surge of LH (luteinizing hormone). This LH surge causes the main (dominant) follicle to release its egg from the ovary (ovulation). Think of LH as a hormone that spurs your reproductive system into action – it stimulates the ovary to produce more progesterone, which is a hormone that is important in fertility and pregnancy.

The egg then travels into the fallopian tube, where it might meet a sperm and become fertilized. If fertilization doesn't happen, the egg eventually dissolves. During ovulation, some people feel a little pain or cramping on one side of their lower belly.

During the menstrual cycle, the rise in oestrogen (for example around ovulation) can make your ligaments (the stretchy bands that hold joints together) a bit looser. This extra flexibility might sound like a good thing, but it can also make joints less stable, which increases the risk of injuries like ankle sprains or even knee problems, especially during sports. That's why some girls are more prone to injury at certain times in their cycle. The England women's football team have also noted higher rates of knee ligament injury compared to male footballers – across all sports, female athletes have around two to eight times the rate of knee ligament injuries!

PHASE 4: Luteal Phase (day 15–28)

After the egg is released, the empty follicle turns into a structure called the corpus luteum. The corpus luteum starts making progesterone, which keeps the endometrium thick in case a fertilized egg needs to stick to the lining of the uterus and grow into a pregnancy. The main focus of your cycle is releasing eggs with the chance of getting pregnant – even though most girls will have roughly **400 periods** over their lifetime and might only choose to have maybe 1 or 2 pregnancies in that time.

If the egg isn't fertilized, the **corpus luteum** (the empty sack in the ovary where the egg came from) breaks down after about 14 days. This makes the progesterone and oestrogen levels drop again – and that drop is what causes the next period to start. The lining of the womb (uterus) isn't needed, so it leaves the body through the vagina. This will be your period. On the first day of your period, the cycle starts all over again. That is why it is called the menstrual cycle – because it starts again as soon as it is over from the month before.

WHY DOES BLEEDING HAPPEN?

Hopefully, all of this has explained a little bit more about what the bleeding part of your menstrual cycle actually is. It is just your body releasing the thickened uterine lining. Along with the endometrial lining, a bit of blood, tissue and mucus pass through the vagina over several days. **It's as simple as that!**

WILL MY PERIODS GO ON FOREVER?

No. In your adult life periods will become part of normal day-to-day living – but they don't carry on forever. Most women stop having periods by around **50 years** of age – this is called **the menopause**. Your periods will slow down over a few years and the hormones that control them will gradually reduce. The menopause is said to have happened when you have not had a period for a year. Many women find going through the menopause much harder than starting their periods in the first place! Historically, the menopause wasn't spoken about much and, a bit like periods, some people felt ashamed or embarrassed to say they were going through the menopause. Luckily this is changing, and many more people are open about going through the menopause and their own experiences. A bit like periods, everyone has their own journey and there is lots of help and support as you go through yours.

When women are pregnant they don't have periods, their bodies stop making eggs because they already have a baby growing in the uterus. Often breastfeeding can stop or slow down your periods, as your body is trying to focus on providing for the baby that you are feeding. Also, some methods of **contraception** (methods of preventing pregnancy) involve taking hormones that make your body think you are pregnant so you stop producing eggs and this can stop you having periods. So, some people will have a period every month for roughly **35–40 years**, but others will have considerable breaks depending on how many children they have or other factors including contraception.

Back in the past, women had way fewer periods than most do today. This wasn't because their bodies were different, but because their lifestyles were. Women often spent more years pregnant or breastfeeding, which naturally paused their cycles. They also started having children earlier and had more of them **(an average of 5–7 pregnancies per woman in Victorian times)**, so their bodies had fewer periods overall. Today, women experience many more periods in their lifetime than women centuries ago.

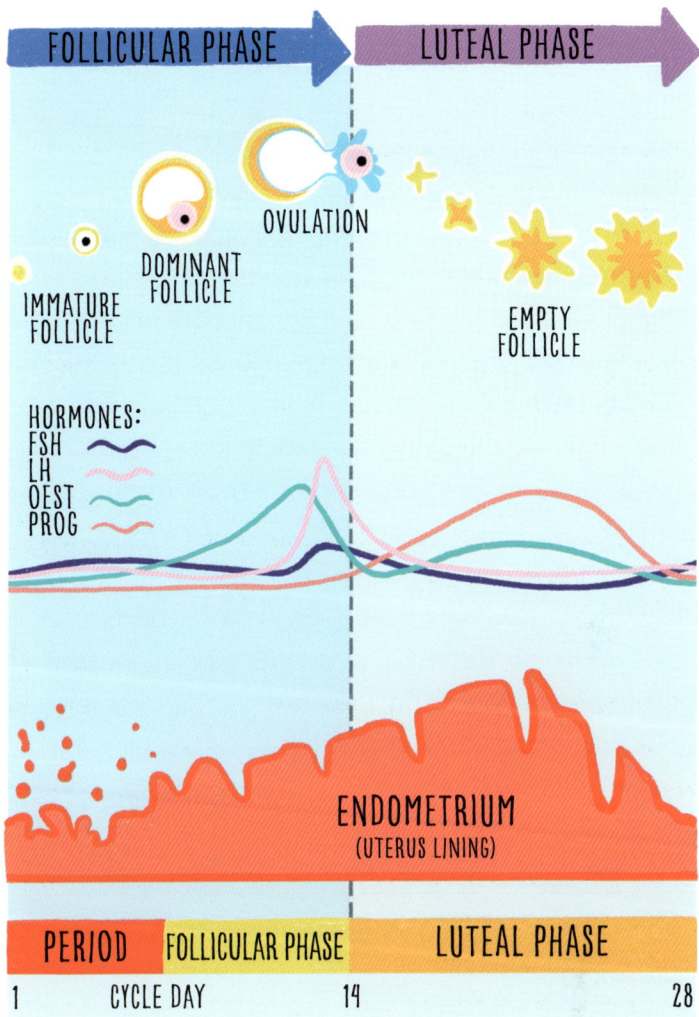

FOLLICULAR PHASE

LUTEAL PHASE

OVULATION

IMMATURE FOLLICLE

DOMINANT FOLLICLE

EMPTY FOLLICLE

HORMONES:
FSH
LH
OEST
PROG

ENDOMETRIUM
(UTERUS LINING)

PERIOD FOLLICULAR PHASE LUTEAL PHASE

1   CYCLE DAY   14   28

This diagram shows a few different things happening throughout your cycle: how the **egg matures** and is released, how the levels of the **four hormones** we've talked about go up and down, and also how the **lining of the womb** changes in thickness.

Ovulation and **periods** are normal parts of the menstrual cycle, controlled by changing levels of hormones like **oestrogen**, **progesterone**, **FSH** and **LH**. Ovulation is when an egg is released from the ovary, and the period is when the body sheds the lining of the uterus if no pregnancy has happened. Even though hormones can make your body feel a bit all over the place sometimes, they're doing important work to keep your **reproductive system** healthy.

Understanding what's going on in your body can help you feel more **confident** and **prepared** each month, and remember, everyone's periods are a little different – but they all follow the same pattern.

YOUR FIRST PERIOD: WHAT TO EXPECT

There are loads of different words and phrases people use to talk about getting their period. Some are a bit weird, some are clever, and some are just funny! You might hear:

- THE TIME OF THE MONTH
- COMING ON
- MOON TIME
- MONTHLY VISITOR
- CODE RED
- MENSTRUATION
- THE PAINTERS ARE IN
- SURFING THE CRIMSON WAVE
- A VISIT FROM AUNT FLO

AUNT FLO

No matter what you call it, having a period can be a bit of a **PAIN** – literally and emotionally – but it's a completely normal part of life.

Everyone's periods arrive at different ages. It is not easy to predict exactly when you are going to start your periods – but the sorts of clues to look out for include other signs of puberty starting, how tall you are and how much you weigh, and what ages your dad went into puberty and your mum started getting her period.

If you feel like the smallest person in the class and it seems like *everyone else* is growing boobs, getting taller or already dealing with their periods, don't panic. It might feel like you're being left behind, **but you're not**.

Think of it a bit like the story of the hare and the tortoise. The hare sets off fast, confident he's going to win, while the **slow-but-steady** tortoise keeps going at his own pace. In the end, it's the tortoise who crosses the finish line first by finally catching up and overtaking the speedy hare. Going through puberty can feel a lot like that, but remember: it's not a competition. Some people start early and seem way ahead, but even if you feel like you're way behind, you'll still get there eventually.

The most important thing to remember? **Puberty isn't a race**, and there's no 'right' time to go through it. Everyone's body has its own schedule, and yours is doing exactly what it's supposed to. As a rough guide, most girls start their periods around the age of 12, but some may start as early as 8 years old, or as late as 15.

HOW WILL I KNOW WHEN MY PERIOD IS ABOUT TO START FOR THE FIRST TIME?

It's hard to predict exactly when your first period will arrive, most people are caught off guard. But there are signs your body gives you that can help you know it might be on the way, so you can be prepared:

- **A white or clear discharge in your underwear**
- **Your breasts starting to grow or feel sore**
- **Hair growing in your armpits and pubic area**

Once you start noticing these changes, your first period will likely arrive within a year or so. Most girls will have a significant amount of pubic hair and moderately advanced breast development before they start their periods. When you reach this phase, it's a good idea to start keeping pads, tampons or your preferred period product in your bag, and maybe even practise using them, so you're not stressed when the day comes.

WHAT TO EXPECT

When your period starts, you'll probably notice blood in your underwear or on the toilet paper when you wipe.

It can be a bit surprising at first, but it's not coming from a cut or wound, so it won't hurt like a scrape would.

Your period is a **sign that your body is working exactly the way it should**, it's not something gross or embarrassing. Without periods, none of us would be here! So while it might feel personal or private (which is totally okay), there's nothing wrong or weird about it.

You might choose to keep it private or only tell a few trusted people, like a parent or close friend. That's up to you. But remember: if you ever need support, there's nothing wrong with letting someone know you've got your period. People understand that it can be a bit of a hassle sometimes, and it's easier when you don't have to hide it.

When your period first starts, you might notice that you only bleed lightly for a few days, and most people find that their period isn't particularly regular for the first few months or even for up to two years after you first start. This is because your body is just getting used to having periods and it can take a bit of time for the hormones to be released in a completely **regular** pattern every month. After a few months, things should settle down and most people would expect a period every 21 to 35 days, with each bleed lasting from a couple of days up to a week. The average number of days between day 1 of each period **(called the cycle length)** is 28 days, and the average length of bleeding is 2 to 7 days – but there is a range, and in time you will get to know and understand your own cycle.

When you feel confident managing your period, like knowing what products work for you, how to avoid leaks and what helps with cramps, it becomes just one part of life, not something that controls it. Most people develop a fairly regular cycle, so once you have started your periods and settled into a regular pattern they should become fairly predictable.

MYTH BUSTING!

MYTH: Periods are gross.
FACT: Nope. They're just your body having its monthly cycle. Totally normal, not shameful, not embarrassing.

MYTH: You lose a lot of blood.
FACT: The average amount is only a few tablespoons per cycle. Sometimes it just seems more than it actually is.

MYTH: You can't swim or play sports.
FACT: This is false! With the right products (tampons, cups or period swimwear), or even without anything (see page 103) you can jump into the pool or power through P.E.

MYTH: Periods = non-stop mood swings.
FACT: Hormones might cause ups and downs in your moods or emotions, but not everyone turns into a walking meltdown. In fact, teenagers

may be less likely to get PMS (premenstrual syndrome) than adults. A study of women and teenagers in the UK found that in every 1,000 girls aged 12–14 years, only around one of them would be diagnosed with PMS by their GP each year. As people get older, they may be more likely to get PMS, but the numbers aren't as high as you might think.

MYTH: Periods are dirty.
FACT: Actually, period blood is just blood – clean and natural. Your body knows what it's doing.

MYTH: Your monthly cycle is only when you are bleeding.
FACT: Wrong! The menstrual cycle is about 28 days long, and includes lots more than just bleeding – such as ovulation (when an egg is released). Your body is doing behind-the-scenes science all month long.

MYTH: You make new eggs every month.
FACT: Nope! You are born with all the eggs you'll ever have – up to two million at birth, though most won't ever be used. Amazingly, before you are born (while you are growing inside your mum) you have even more eggs in your ovaries – more than 5 million!

MANAGING MENSTRUATION: PRODUCTS & PRACTICES

When you're on your period, you'll need to use something to stop the blood leaking onto your underwear or clothes. The amount of blood you lose during your period does vary – but it tends to be heavier (more blood loss) at the beginning than the end of your period, so you may use different things on different days of your period. There are a few options... so let's learn some more!

SANITARY TOWELS (PADS)

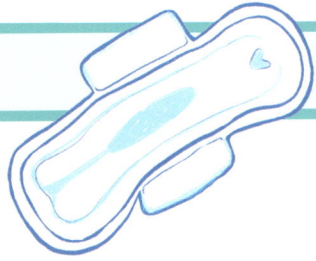

Most people use pads when they first start their periods because they're super simple at a time when you're getting used to your period. They are essentially a thin pad that you stick to the inside of your pants to absorb the blood so it doesn't leak onto your underwear or clothes.

Pads come in different **shapes** and **thicknesses**. At the start of your period or at night you might need a bigger, thicker pad, and then you might want to switch to a thinner one when the bleeding gets lighter near the end. Throughout your period, you will need to change the pad every **4–6 hours** depending on the heaviness of your bleed. You can also buy pantyliners for very light flow, these are thinner and smaller than pads.

Pads are a great option, especially when you have just started your period, but there are a few downsides. They can be expensive, especially when you add up the cost of 4–6 pads a day for roughly a week out of each month, for many years! Also they are not great for the environment, as you just throw them in the bin when you have used one.

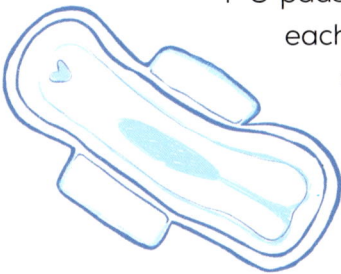

DISPOSING OF PADS

Pretty much all public toilets have a **sanitary bin** where you can put your used pad – you lift the lid and pop it on a little tray and it disappears when you close it. Remember, sanitary towels **can't be flushed away** or you will block the loo, so you do need to make sure you dispose of your pads properly. If they do get flushed, they will end up in rivers and oceans contributing to pollution and affecting wildlife – so they definitely need to go into a sanitary bin, **NOT** down the loo! Most families will have a small bin in their bathroom for pads, and it is best to wrap the pad in some loo roll or in a disposable plastic bag before binning.

REUSABLE PADS

These days there are also **reusable pads** that you can pop in the wash rather than binning each time. Although these are more expensive than buying the disposable pads, you will save the money long-term as you can **reuse** them over and over again. They are made of various materials like **cotton** or **bamboo**. Washing reusable cloth pads can be straightforward and hygienic, not to mention better for the environment. It is best to first rinse them in cold water, ideally as soon as possible after using – or to soak them overnight. Don't wring them out, but squeeze gently to get rid of excess water. Change the water daily if soaking for longer than 12 hours. The pads can then be hand or machine washed on a normal 30 or 40°C wash. It is best to air dry the pads as tumble drying may reduce the lifespan over time.

AVOID:
- **Fabric softener:** reduces absorbency
- **Bleach:** weakens the fabric and irritates the skin
- **Ironing:** damages the waterproof layer
- **Harsh detergents or antibacterial soaps:** will irritate sensitive skin

PAD PROS
- **Very easy to use** – just stick them onto your underwear
- **No risk of toxic shock syndrome** (TSS, see page 46 for more info)
- **Lots of sizes and absorbencies** to suit heavy or light days

PAD CONS
- Can feel **bulky** or **uncomfortable**, especially during sports
- Can be more **noticeable** under tight clothes
- Need to be **changed often**, and can sometimes cause **odours** if worn too long
- Disposable pads **aren't environmentally friendly**

TAMPONS

Tampons are small, tube-shaped products made of soft, absorbent material, with a string on the end. Unlike pads which sit outside of your body, they go **inside** your vagina and soak up period blood from the inside. It can take a little practice to get used to using them, but once you've figured it out, they're actually pretty easy. There are some big **bonuses** with tampons which is why some people prefer to use them – for example they can make it **easier** to wear certain clothes or to exercise or swim. They can be more **comfortable** compared to a pad being in your underwear which can get a bit messy or feel unpleasant if left without changing for too long. Tampons are generally quite **discreet** as you just remove them when you go to the toilet and pop them in the bin – just like sanitary pads they should **not** be flushed down the loo. **TOP TIP:** keep a small sealable disposable bag with you for discreet disposal when you're out. Whether you use pads or tampons is a matter of personal choice, and lots of people use both at different times and for different reasons.

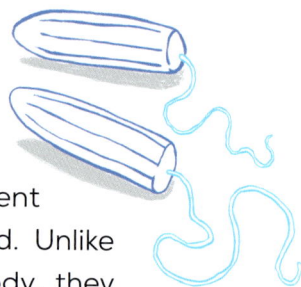

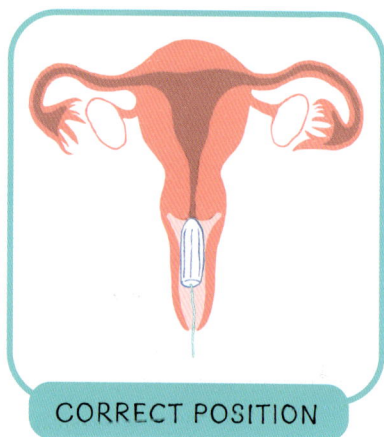

CORRECT POSITION

The key to making a tampon feel comfortable is putting it in far enough. If it's not sitting high enough, it'll feel awkward and uncomfortable. But when it's in the right spot, you shouldn't feel it at all.

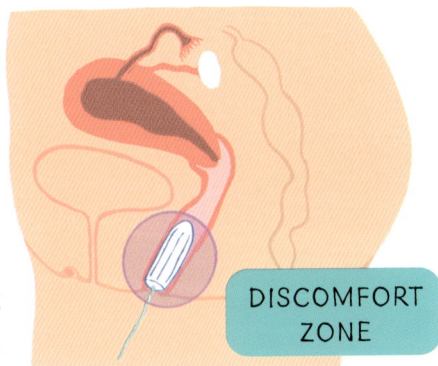

DISCOMFORT ZONE

Some tampons come with an **applicator** to help you insert them more easily. Others you insert using your finger, which might take a bit of getting used to (see page 44 for more detailed instructions). **Just be gentle** – your skin is delicate down there! Why not try both types at home to see which one you prefer? Your mum or a close family member or friend might be able to give you advice and talk you through using a tampon to help you decide whether you would like to try using them.

A bit like with pads, you need to use the **right tampon** depending on how heavy your period is. For example, on the first day or two you might need a tampon which is a bit bigger and more absorbent, then as your period goes on you can use a smaller tampon. They come in **different sizes** which are usually shown on the outside of the packaging. Some brands might use words like 'super' or 'super plus' for the bigger tampons, and 'regular' or 'light' for the smaller tampons. These sizes aren't describing the size of you, but the **heaviness of the flow**. You will get used to the different sizes and when you might need to use each one. Some brands sell a single packet with a range of tampon sizes so you can choose the right one for each day as your period progresses.

Something really important to know is that you need to change your tampon regularly. This usually means every **4–6 hours**, or when the tampon is full. You usually know when the tampon is full because you might leak a little bit, notice blood on the string coming down, or feel like the tampon is starting to come out. If your period is quite heavy you might need to change it more often. You can wear a tampon overnight, but you should insert it just before you go to bed and change it as soon as you wake up.

Always use the smallest tampon for your flow – for example if you are nearing the end of your period, switch to a smaller tampon and don't keep using the larger ones. Or, if your tampon hasn't absorbed very much blood when you take it out, try a smaller one. If your period is very heavy, it's okay to wear a tampon and a pad or pantyliner together for **extra protection**. Some people find they need to use a tampon and a pad together, especially at the beginning of their period, and that is not unusual, but if that happens often, it might be a good idea to chat with your doctor.

A bit like pads, tampons are also not very environmentally

friendly as you need to dispose of them in the bin, and obviously you can only use each tampon once.

HOW TO INSERT A TAMPON

It might sound scary, but putting a tampon in is **super easy!** At first it can take some practice, but once you get the hang of it you can do it without even thinking.

It might sound silly, but the first thing to do is take a tampon out of its wrapper and **have a look**. If you have one with an applicator (a cardboard or plastic tube) then work out how the tampon fits inside the applicator and how to push it out. It's good to be really familiar with how a tampon works, to help you work out how to put it in properly. They will usually come with instructions, so have a good read if there is anything you aren't sure about. Going through it with an adult can be really helpful too.

The second thing to be familiar with is where the tampon is **going**. That means finding your **vaginal opening** – this can be tricky the first time! Sometimes having a look with a **mirror** or a feel with your (clean) fingers can be helpful as it is low down between your legs and is generally tricky to see. Don't be embarrassed, this is your body! It's almost impossible to put the tampon in the wrong place,

but having a good look down there to see what you are aiming for is very helpful.

Once you are familiar with the product you are using and your own anatomy, it's time to give it a try. Everyone will do it slightly differently but here are some top tips:

1   Wash your hands. It's always a good idea to have clean hands to reduce the risk of infection.

2   Get in a comfy position. This is very individual, but some people find it helpful to put one foot on the toilet seat, or squat slightly with their knees apart.

3   Tilt the tampon slightly backwards in the direction of your lower back – not straight up towards your belly. This helps the tampon to follow the direction that your vagina naturally goes in, so will make it more comfortable (see diagram on page 40).

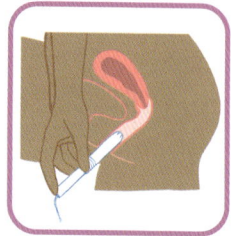

4   Follow the instructions on the packet to make sure you get the tampon far enough inside. If you can feel the tampon after you have inserted it, that probably means it's not

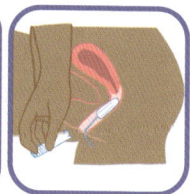

quite far enough. Use your index finger to try pushing it a little further in, or just remove it and start again.

5   If you have any pain or discomfort – stop! It shouldn't hurt. Maybe have a little break, relax your body, and then try again. Or speak to an adult you can trust for advice, have another look at the instructions or maybe try another day! You can always use pads until you feel confident to give it another try.

6   **Finally** – dispose of the rubbish. Wrap the applicator in its packaging or toilet tissue and put it in the bin, and when you have finished with your tampon, pop that in the bin, too. You can also wrap it in a little loo paper or use a disposable sanitary bag if you want to.

STAYING FRESH AND SAFE WITH TAMPONS

Whatever product you use, it's important to change it regularly. If your period is heavier **(more blood)**, you'll need to change more often. Periods usually last between **2 and 7 days**, and they're often heaviest in the first couple of days. At the start, you might need to change your pad or tampon every few hours, maybe **4–5 times a day**.

Tampons should be changed every **4–6 hours** or so, and not be left in for more than 8 hours. Leaving one in too long can cause a rare but serious infection called toxic shock syndrome **(TSS)**.

TSS is caused by certain **bacteria** that can grow and release harmful toxins into your body. While it is rare, it's important to know the risks so you can protect yourself. Using super-absorbent tampons when you don't need them or forgetting to change your tampon regularly (at least every 4 to 8 hours) can raise your chances of getting TSS. To help you remember, try setting a phone reminder, you could even set it with a code name like **'Red Alert!'**.

Signs of TSS include a sudden **high fever**, **feeling dizzy** or **faint**, **vomiting**, **diarrhoea**, **a rash** that looks like sunburn, and **muscle aches**. If you ever feel really unwell while using a tampon, it's important to take it out right away and tell an adult or see a doctor. TSS can get serious quickly, but if it's caught early, it can be treated easily. To stay safe, always use the lowest absorbency you need, don't leave tampons in for too long, or you could switch to pads or period pants at night. Knowing the signs and taking small steps can help keep you healthy and confident during your period. TSS is very rare – only about **1 or 2 cases occur in every 100,000 women in the UK** – but it can be serious, so knowing about the risks and the signs can help make sure it never happens to you.

TAMPON PROS

- **Small and discreet**, easy to carry in your bag or pocket.
- **Great for sports**, swimming and active days.
- Once inserted correctly, **you won't feel it** inside your body at all.

TAMPON CONS

- Can be tricky to **learn how to insert** at first.
- Need to be changed every 4–8 hours to stay safe and comfortable, with **very rare but serious risk of TSS** if worn too long.
- **Not environmentally friendly.**

PERIOD PANTS

Period pants (also called period underwear) are a type of **reusable underwear** specially designed to **absorb** blood during your period. They look and feel like regular underwear but have built-in layers of fabric that soak up your period without the need for pads or tampons. They have a **hidden absorbent panel** where you would usually stick a pad. This means you don't need to use a pad or tampon, but can just wear these comfy pants and go out without worrying.

HOW DO PERIOD PANTS WORK?

Period pants have multiple layers in the crotch area. The inner layer closest to your skin usually absorbs liquid quickly, so you **feel dry**. The middle layers are super absorbent and hold the blood. The outer layer is leak-proof to stop any blood from soaking through to your clothes. Depending on the brand and style, period pants can absorb the same amount as between 1 to 6 tampons' worth of blood. There is a choice of **different absorbencies** to suit your flow.

HOW TO USE PERIOD PANTS

Using period pants is easy. You just put them on like **regular underwear**. When they're full – or at the end of the day – you take them off and rinse them in cold water first to remove the blood. Rinse them until the water runs clear. After rinsing, you can either hand-wash them or put them in the washing machine (check the label for your particular brand's instructions). Just make sure you don't use fabric softener, as this will affect the future absorbency of the pants. They need to air dry – no tumble dryers, as heat can damage the absorbent layers. It's a good idea to speak to an adult about the way you plan to organize rinsing, washing and drying them during your period, so that they can give you a hand.

Some people wear period pants all day, while others use them as backup with tampons or menstrual cups (see page 51). You might need to change them during the day if you have a heavy flow. Many teens find them **perfect for school days or bedtime** because you don't need to worry about leaks or changing pads or tampons every few hours.

PERIOD PANT PROS

- **Comfort:** they feel just like normal underwear – no bulky pads or strings.
- **Eco-friendly:** they're reusable, so they create less waste than disposable products and are therefore better for the planet.
- **Cost-effective:** though more expensive upfront compared to buying a box of tampons or pads, they save money over time since you can reuse them for years.
- **Discreet:** no crinkling pad sounds. Great for P.E or sleepovers.
- **Easy for beginners:** no need to learn how to insert anything like tampons or menstrual cups.

PERIOD PANT CONS

- **Upfront cost:** one pair can cost more than a box of pads or tampons, and you'll need several to get through a full cycle.
- **Washing required:** you need to rinse and wash them, which some people find unpleasant or inconvenient.

- **Changing at school:** if you need to change them during the day, you'll need a waterproof bag to carry the used pair home.
- **Drying time:** they take a while to air dry after washing, especially the thicker ones.

DIFFERENT VARIETIES OF PERIOD PANTS

There are many styles to suit different flows and preferences:

- **Light flow:** thinner pants designed for the start or end of your period. The equivalent of 1–2 tampons.
- **Medium flow:** this will absorb about 2–3 tampons worth, which is about typical for an average period each day.
- **Heavy flow:** more absorbent pairs with extra layers. The equivalent of 4–6 tampons, but if you have a much heavier flow you can get super absorbent varieties.
- **Overnight:** full-coverage styles that are leak-proof and great for sleeping.
- **Sporty styles:** designed for movement, great for P.E. or dance class.
- **High-waisted or bikini styles:** just like your underwear, they come in different cuts and fits to suit all shapes, sizes and preferences.

Period pants are a **modern**, **easy** and **comfortable** way to manage your period. They're especially helpful for people who want something **fuss-free**, and they can help you feel more confident during your period. If you're curious, try one pair first to see how you like them – you might end up never going back to pads or tampons!

MENSTRUAL CUP

A menstrual cup (**or period cup**) is a safe, **eco-friendly** and **cost-effective** alternative to pads and tampons. It is a small, flexible cup, usually made of **medical grade silicone**, **rubber** or **thermoplastic elastomer** (a type of plastic that feels like rubber). These materials are safe for your body and designed to be **reusable** for several years if cared for properly. Be careful to check the material that your menstrual cup is made of – for example if you are allergic to latex, don't choose a rubber cup!

A menstrual cup is inserted into the vagina, where it **collects** the blood instead of absorbing it like tampons or pads. Once inside, it creates a seal against the vaginal walls, preventing leaks. Most cups can hold more blood than tampons, so you may only need to empty them 2 to 4 times a day, depending on your flow.

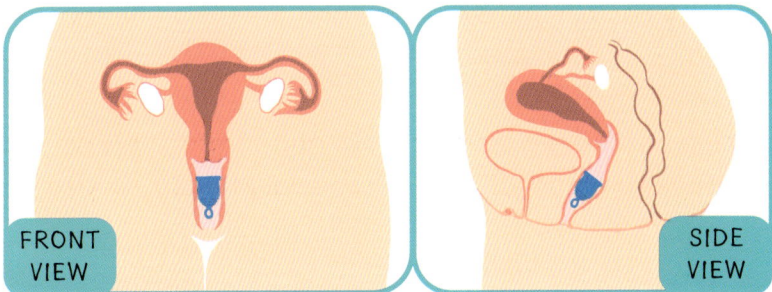

FRONT VIEW

SIDE VIEW

HOW TO USE A MENSTRUAL CUP:

1. **Wash your hands** thoroughly before handling the cup.
2. **Fold the cup** (there are different fold techniques, like the C-fold or punch-down fold) and gently insert it into the vagina.
3. **Let it unfold** inside so it can create a seal. You might need to twist it slightly or run a finger around the base to ensure it's properly opened.
4. **After up to 6 to 12 hours, remove the cup** by pinching the base to release the seal, then pull it out gently.
5. **Empty the contents** into the toilet, **rinse the cup**, and reinsert it.

At the end of your period, sterilize the cup by boiling it in water for 5–10 minutes and store it in a breathable bag.

Trying a menstrual cup for the first time can feel awkward, but it gets easier with practice. They're great for active lifestyles, swimming and even sleeping. Menstrual cups might not be the thing for you when you first start your periods, but they are a really environmentally-friendly period product, and lots of women switch to them when they are a little older and more experienced at managing their periods. One of the things to remember when thinking about using a menstrual cup is that you would ideally only use one when you have access to a private sink inside the toilet cubicle so that you can rinse the cup and wash your hands with some privacy – so a menstrual cup may not be ideal when you are going to school or if you might need to empty the cup in a public toilet with shared sink facilities.

MENSTRUAL CUP PROS

- **Eco-friendly and reusable** – can last for years, so saves money.
- **Can be worn for up to 6–12 hours**, even overnight.
- **Holds more blood** than pads or tampons, so fewer changes needed.

MENSTRUAL CUP CONS

- **Can take practice** to insert and remove comfortably
- **Need to be rinsed and sterilized**, which isn't always easy in public bathrooms.
- Some people may feel **squeamish** about touching blood during emptying.

TRACKING AND UNDERSTANDING YOUR CYCLE

As we have already mentioned, when you first start getting your period, it might be a bit all over the place. You could bleed one month, then not get anything for a few months, and then it shows up again. Don't worry, this is totally normal at the beginning. Over time, your period will most likely settle into a more regular pattern. It's a smart idea to keep track of when each period starts using a calendar or a period tracking app, so you can get a rough idea of when to expect the next one. That way you can be prepared, and it won't catch you off guard. Most people get their period every 28 days or so, but anything between 21 and 35 days is normal too.

The length of your cycle can **vary** in the first few months after starting your period, and so can the length of your period **(the number of days you are bleeding for)**. On one occasion you might bleed for three days, then the next time seven days. This is very normal, although it can be slightly annoying if you are trying to plan or predict your periods. Remember that your body is getting used to something new, and this takes time, just like trying to learn a new skill! You have to be a little bit **patient** and just wait for things to settle down. Tracking your period is a really good way of monitoring if your period is settling down. If they are still irregular a couple of years after starting your periods, it may be worth discussing that with your GP.

Lots of people find it really helpful to **track their period each month**. You can then start to get a good idea of when your cycle might start, and how many days you might bleed for. This can be really useful when it comes to planning things like activities, sleepovers or holidays, and making sure you are being **prepared** with sanitary products.

There are quite a few ways of doing this. You could simply make a note on a calendar or in a diary of when your period starts and ends. You could also include information about how heavy it was, or any other symptoms you experienced if you want to. For example, you might want to make note of how your body is feeling in areas like:

HEADACHES

BACKACHE

ENERGY LEVELS

HOW WELL
YOU SLEPT
LAST NIGHT

TUMMY
ISSUES

APPETITE

DISCHARGE

SORE BOOBS

You might also want to make a note of how you are feeling **mentally** or **emotionally**. Sometimes these feelings can be tricky to name, so here's a list you might want to refer to if you're struggling:

STRONG

ANXIOUS

FRUSTRATED

WORRIED

ANGRY

TEARY

QUIET

ENERGIZED

RESTLESS

PEACEFUL

JEALOUS

CONFUSED

SCATTERED

IRRITABLE

EXCITED

SAD

HAPPY

CONTENT

WEAK

FOCUSED

PRODUCTIVE

Some people find that as their **hormones go up and down** in each phase over their cycle, they notice changes in the way they **feel** and **think**. For example, you might find that you feel more **energetic** at certain times during your cycle, or your appetite might change at others. You might feel your mood is a bit **up and down**. The way we feel and think during our monthly cycle varies from one person to another, and you will probably find that it even varies for you from month to month! So don't worry if you feel different during one month compared to another, and certainly don't worry about experiencing different things to your friends and family. The most important thing to do is to **track your symptoms** such as **mood**, **energy levels**, **sleep** or **appetite** to help you **take control** of your cycle and be able to predict how you might feel in each phase. If you don't have any symptoms that bother you, you might feel you don't need to write anything down, or you might find it interesting to monitor over the months. **It's totally up to you.**

There are plenty of **apps** available specifically for recording your monthly cycle. They often have easy ways of **logging** when your period starts, and even **reminding you** that your period might be coming in the next few days, which is very handy. **This can be helpful if you have regular or irregular periods.**

Tracking your period can also help you notice any **patterns** or **symptoms** that you might want to seek advice about, for example if your periods are very irregular **(your cycle length changes from month to month)**, very heavy, or if you are bleeding for a different number of days each month. You might also notice an impact on your **mood**, **energy levels**, **appetite** or **general wellbeing** that seems related to your periods. Without making a note of things, it can be hard to remember exactly what happens from month to month – especially between school, clubs and your social life! Also, if you have kept track of your cycle and you want to seek help from your doctor, they will find it super helpful being able to see everything you have recorded, so it really is a **win-win**.

One of the final reasons it is helpful to track your periods accurately is so that you can **predict** – and maybe even **plan** – what to do if you are going to have a period at an important time – for example during a big family holiday or a school camping trip. If it becomes clear that your period is due at a time when it will be really annoying, it is possible to **delay** your period. This is not something that is suggested to do frequently in young girls or teenagers, but can be done by taking a short course of human-made progesterone (called **norethisterone**). You start this three days before your period is due and can continue taking it for as long as you need to delay your period, up to a maximum of 17 days. You would need to see your GP to discuss this and get a **prescription**. The GP might recommend waiting until your periods have settled and you have a more regular routine before taking any medication like this.

DEALING WITH DISCOMFORT: CRAMPS AND PREMENSTRUAL SYNDROME

Getting your period is a normal part of growing up, but that doesn't mean it always feels easy. For many young people, periods come with a mix of physical and emotional changes. You might have cramps, feel emotional or notice that your body feels different to usual. These things can be uncomfortable – but there are ways to deal with them, and you're definitely not alone.

Quite apart from the practical issues relating to the blood loss, girls can experience extra physical symptoms or sometimes mood and emotional changes in the run up to a period, or during a period.

Two of the most common period-related discomforts are **cramps** and **PMS**, or premenstrual syndrome. Pre is just the medical way of saying **'before'** – so premenstrual syndrome is just the medical term for the emotions, mood swings and physical symptoms that you might experience before your period. We think these are due to the hormone changes that happen in the week before your period begins.

Cramps usually feel like a **pain** in your lower belly or back, and can be **sharp** (like a twisting sensation) or **dull** (like an ache). Sometimes this discomfort can spread to your upper belly or thighs. These are caused by **muscles in your uterus tightening** to shed the lining of the uterus, which is what causes bleeding during your period. These **tightenings** can be uncomfortable, especially on the first couple of days of your period, or for a day or two before it starts.

PMS happens in the days leading up to your period. It's when you might feel more emotional than usual – maybe you get irritated easily, feel sad or anxious, or have mood swings. You might also notice other signs like **headaches**, **acne**, **bloating** (feeling your tummy is a bit bigger than usual), **sore breasts**, **fancying certain foods**, **feeling tired**, or having trouble sleeping. PMS is caused by changes in your hormone levels, especially oestrogen and progesterone, which naturally rise and fall during your cycle (see the diagram on page 27).

You are unlikely to experience all of these symptoms every month, and some months might feel worse than others. Research suggests that about half of girls and young adults experience some symptoms in the run up to their period – the good news is that these symptoms tend to be less noticeable when you first start your periods, so you may not notice anything at all.

WAYS TO FEEL BETTER

There's no magic way to make periods completely pain-free, but there are a lot of things you can do to feel better. Check out these suggestions – some are natural options, and some involve things like taking pain killers. These tips can help you manage cramps, mood swings and other PMS symptoms:

1 **Use heat:** a warm heating pad or hot water bottle on your lower belly can help relax the muscles that cause cramps. A warm bath can help too.

2 **Massage:** gently rubbing your tummy or lower back can really be soothing when you have period pain. You could use a little bit of warm oil or lotion if you prefer, or even do it when you are in the bath for extra comfort.

3 **Move your body:** exercise might be the last thing you want to do, but gentle activities like walking, stretching or yoga can actually help reduce cramps and boost your mood by releasing feel-good hormones called endorphins.

4 **Eat balanced meals:** try to eat regular meals with fruits, vegetables, whole grains (like oats, brown rice and whole grain bread) and protein. Basically, trying to keep your body fuelled with lots of nutrients and vitamins is always a good idea.

5 **Drink water:** staying hydrated can help prevent bloating and eases cramps. A bit like eating a balanced diet, keeping our bodies hydrated is generally a great way to look after our physical and mental health, period or not!

6 **Get plenty of sleep:** your body needs rest, especially during your period. Try to stick to a regular bedtime and wind down before sleep by turning off screens and doing something relaxing, like reading or listening to music.

7 **Try herbal remedies:** some people find using natural remedies like ginger tea or chamomile tea can be calming and relaxing. Always ask a parent, guardian or doctor before trying any new supplements or teas.

8 **Consider trying pain killers:** if you feel like none of these suggestions are helpful, you could try simple pain killers such as paracetamol or ibuprofen. These can be bought in a pharmacy without needing a prescription from your doctor, but it's very important to get help and advice from an adult before taking any medication. Please don't do it by yourself, and always follow the recommended dosage given in the instructions inside the box. Simple pain relievers such as ibuprofen are extremely helpful in treating period pain – they not only help with pain symptoms but also have an important role in helping with heavy periods. Taking regular ibuprofen around the time your period is due can reduce the amount of flow by as much as a third. If your periods are so heavy that you are thinking of trying regular ibuprofen, you should see your GP beforehand to discuss it, there might be other possible ways of making things easier for you.

9 **Remember to track your cycle:** writing down or using an app to track your period and symptoms can help you notice patterns. That way, you can be prepared and know what to expect next time.

WHEN TO TALK TO A DOCTOR

While some discomfort is totally normal, you should always talk to a trusted adult or a doctor if:

YOU FEEL DIZZY, WEAK OR FAINT DURING YOUR PERIOD.

YOUR CRAMPS ARE SO PAINFUL THAT YOU CAN'T GO TO SCHOOL OR DO REGULAR ACTIVITIES.

WHEN TO TALK TO THE DOCTOR

YOUR PERIOD LASTS LONGER THAN 7 DAYS, OR YOU BLEED SO MUCH THAT YOU HAVE TO CHANGE YOUR PAD OR TAMPON EVERY 1-2 HOURS.

YOU FEEL VERY SAD, ANGRY OR OUT OF CONTROL AROUND YOUR PERIOD.

DAY 1 → DAY 7

In some cases, intense period pain could be a sign of a condition like **endometriosis** or **polycystic ovary syndrome (PCOS)**, which need medical attention (check out When Things Aren't Normal on page 105 for more information). If something doesn't feel right, it's okay to ask for help.

Non-drug treatments like **exercise, good sleep, healthy food** and other **stress-reducing activities** can make PMS much easier to handle. Every person is different, so it may take a little experimenting to see what works best for you.

If your symptoms are still not manageable, or are significantly affecting your day-to-day life, then think about going to see your GP, they will probably have further advice or treatments they can offer you. In the most difficult cases, other treatments such as a trial of hormonal medicines (for example, '**the pill**') can reduce symptoms, but this is usually reserved for older teenagers rather than when your periods are just starting out.

YOU'RE NOT ALONE

It's easy to feel **embarrassed** or **frustrated** about your period, especially when you're dealing with cramps or mood swings. But periods are something **half the people on the planet experience** – and finding it tricky at times is nothing to be ashamed of. Talking about it with a parent, friend, school nurse or doctor can help you feel more supported and **less stressed.**

REMEMBER: your body is doing something incredible and natural. Learning how to take care of yourself during your period is part of getting to know your body better. As time goes on, you'll figure out what works best for **you**.

EMOTIONAL WELL-BEING AND SELF-CARE

Your period is a **natural** part of growing up. It's something that happens to people all around the world, every single day. But even though it's completely normal, it can bring a mix of emotions, physical changes, and even confusing thoughts.

The good news is, you're not alone, and there are plenty of ways to take care of your emotional well-being and feel your best, even on tough days. Let's talk about how to understand your feelings, practise self-care, and feel confident in your body throughout your cycle.

UNDERSTANDING MOOD SWINGS AND EMOTIONAL CHANGES

Have you ever felt **really sad** for no reason right before your period? Or maybe you felt **super tired** or **annoyed**, or you even **burst into tears** over something small? That's not '**just being dramatic**', those are real symptoms that many people experience during their monthly cycle.

WHY DOES THIS HAPPEN?

It all has to do with **hormones**. Your body produces different hormones throughout the month, and the levels of these hormones go up and down, especially **oestrogen** and **progesterone**. These hormones don't just control your period; they can also affect your brain and **emotions**. Scientists still don't fully understand how and why this happens, but we know that some people are affected more than others. Even if you are someone who doesn't notice much change in your mood around your period, it's good to understand a bit more about it so you can help support others around you.

SELF-CARE ROUTINES DURING MENSTRUATION

Self-care means doing things that help you feel good, stay healthy and take care of your mind and body. During your period your body is working hard, so it's a perfect time to slow down and give yourself extra care.

Here are some simple, gentle self-care ideas to try when you're on your period:

REST AND SLEEP

It's **normal** to feel more tired during your period. Take breaks when your body needs them, you don't have to do everything at once.

Try to get 8–10 hours of sleep each night – **minimum!** All teenagers need increased hours of sleep – you have got all that growing to do! Sleep difficulties are common, and there is lots of extra information available online, but here are a few simple tips for a good night's sleep:

AVOID sugary or energy drinks after lunchtime – these aren't actually good for you at any time of day!

TRY to put your phone or tablet down, and avoid TV for two hours before bed. Scrolling late can make it harder to fall asleep. Screentime reduces your body's production of melatonin (your natural sleep hormone).

AVOID super stimulating stuff in the evening, like intense video games or blasting music. Instead, why not listen to calming music, a podcast or an audio book?

CREATE a wind-down routine that works for you, maybe a warm shower, reading a book, or having a warm (non-caffeinated) drink like milk or herbal tea. Keep your room as dark as possible when you sleep. Darkness tells your brain it's time to release melatonin. Don't go to bed hungry, but avoid heavy snacks right before sleeping too. A light snack earlier in the evening is fine.

COMFORT YOUR BODY

Take time to work out what you find comforting. Some people find using a hot water bottle on their stomach can ease cramps, or taking a warm bath or shower can relax their muscles. Also, it sounds like a small thing, but wearing soft, comfortable clothes can make you feel all snuggly and relaxed. **Yes, your favourite cosy hoodie counts!**

EAT NOURISHING FOODS

It's totally fine to enjoy a treat now and then, especially if you're not feeling great during your period, but keeping your diet balanced most of the time can really help your body feel stronger and more energized.

A balanced diet means having a bit of everything, not loads of one thing. Try to get some fruit and veggies in every day, eat foods with plenty of iron, and cut back on foods that are packed with sugar. It actually makes a difference to how you feel throughout your cycle! Also try not to skip meals, because even if you don't feel super hungry, your body still needs fuel.

Also, **don't forget to drink water**. Your body's made up of mostly water, and staying hydrated helps *everything* – your digestion, your brain, your energy levels, even how well your kidneys work. Basically, water is underrated and very important, especially when your body's going through its cycle each month.

MOVE YOUR BODY GENTLY

Light exercise like stretching, walking or yoga can actually help reduce cramps and boost your mood. You don't need to do anything intense, just a little movement can go a long way.

RELAX YOUR MIND

Like all aspects of self-care, what you find helpful to relax your mind will be individual to you. Some suggestions you could try are listening to your favourite music, reading a book, writing in a journal or watching a feel-good movie or your favourite TV series. Some people also find breathing exercises or meditation helpful, these can take practice but there are loads of helpful apps and resources online. Self-care looks different for everyone. What matters most is choosing things that help you feel peaceful, calm or even a little bit happier.

BUILDING A POSITIVE BODY IMAGE

During puberty, and especially during your period, your body goes through lots of changes. Some days you might feel bloated, get acne or just not feel confident. That's okay, everyone has those days. But it's important to treat your body with kindness, no matter what.

WHAT IS BODY IMAGE?

Body image is how you think and feel about your body, including how it looks and how it works. You might have: **positive body image** – you respect and accept your body. **Negative body image** – you feel ashamed, upset or uncomfortable about how you look.

Most people have a **bit of both** – there are parts of their body they like and accept, and others they are not so fond of, or they have days where they feel good and days where they feel not so good. This is okay, as long as your overall feeling about yourself and your body is positive.

Here are some top tips for boosting body confidence:

1 **Say kind things to yourself**
This might feel strange but try doing it looking in the mirror! See if you can notice things about yourself that you like, and say out loud things like:

'I AM STRONG.'   'I AM A FUNNY AND KIND PERSON.'

'IT'S COMPLETELY NORMAL TO HAVE A PERIOD.'

'I DON'T NEED TO BE PERFECT.'

2 Stop comparing

The media in general, but especially social media can make it seem like everyone looks flawless all the time, but most pictures are filtered, posed or edited. No one looks perfect all the time and that also applies during your period. Comparing yourself to other people is one of the worst things you can do when it comes to self-esteem or body image, because we generally pick out the things about ourselves that we like the least to compare to others. We are all different, unique and special, so comparing ourselves to other people is not only pointless but is a surefire way to make you feel worse overall!

3 Focus on what your body can do

Your body enables you to **dance, run, hug, laugh, cry** and **grow**. That's amazing.

4 Wear what makes you feel good

You don't have to follow trends. Choose clothes that make you feel comfortable and confident, especially while on your period.

5 **Talk about your feelings**

You're not alone. Talking to friends, a trusted adult, a sibling or relative can help you feel better and realize lots of people feel the same way.

DON'T BE AFRAID TO ASK FOR SUPPORT

If you're having a tough day, physically or emotionally, it's okay to ask for help.

YOU MIGHT SAY:

'HEY, I'M FEELING REALLY TIRED TODAY. CAN I REST FOR A BIT?'

'I'VE GOT CRAMPS. DO YOU HAVE A HEAT PACK OR SOME TEA?'

'I'M FEELING EMOTIONAL. CAN WE TALK?'

'CAN YOU HELP ME GET SOME PADS/TAMPONS?'

The people who care about you, like parents, guardians, teachers or friends, want to help. Let them know what you need.

And if you ever feel **overwhelmed**, **worried**, or **really sad** for a long time, it's important to talk to a trusted adult and get some help. You might choose to see your doctor for some advice. Periods can cause mood changes, but if you're feeling down a lot, you may need extra support.

REMEMBER THIS...

Your period doesn't make you any less amazing. It's a sign that your body is **healthy, powerful**, and **doing exactly what it's supposed to. You don't have to hide your period or be embarrassed.**

Self-care isn't selfish, it's smart. Your body is worthy of love and respect, even when it's bloated or tired. You are more than your appearance. You are smart, kind and brave. It's okay to have emotional days, you're allowed to feel!

Taking care of your **emotional well-being** and practising self-care during your period isn't just helpful, it's an act of self-love. And the more you learn about your body, listen to your needs, and support yourself, the stronger and more confident you'll become.

CARING FOR SOMEONE DURING THEIR PERIOD

Most girls will have a period once a month for a big part of their lives. That means, at some point, your friend, sister, cousin, mum or classmate might be dealing with cramps, mood swings, or just feeling off – and they may really appreciate a little extra care and understanding. And don't forget – that includes adults too! Even though adults have had more time than teenagers to get used to periods, they can get similar symptoms to teenagers, such as cramps or feeling up and down with their emotions.

Whether you get a period yourself or not, being kind and helpful to someone who's on theirs is a great way to show support, be a good friend, and be a thoughtful person.

Let's look at how you can offer emotional support, practical help, and just be someone others can count on during this time.

STEP 1: BE UNDERSTANDING

First things first, periods are **totally normal**. They're not weird, shameful or something to joke about. People who get periods aren't being dramatic or moody on purpose, they're dealing with real physical and emotional changes in their bodies.

As we have talked about, during their period or monthly cycle, **someone might feel:**

CRAMPY OR IN PAIN	NERVOUS ABOUT PEOPLE NOTICING	TIRED OR LOW-ENERGY
UPSET, SAD OR EXTRA SENSITIVE	EMBARRASSED ABOUT LEAKS OR NEEDING TO CHANGE PRODUCTS	

Even if you don't fully understand what it feels like, you can still **listen, believe them and be patient**.

HERE'S SOME TOP TIPS FOR HOW TO BE UNDERSTANDING:

DON'T MAKE JOKES ABOUT 'THE TIME OF THE MONTH'.

NEVER TEASE SOMEONE FOR HOW THEY'RE FEELING OR ACTING.

IF SOMEONE TELLS YOU THEY'RE IN PAIN, BELIEVE THEM.

DON'T ACT GROSSED OUT BY PERIODS.

Sometimes, the best thing you can do is just be there and let them know it's okay to talk or ask for help.

STEP 2: OFFER EMOTIONAL SUPPORT

Having your period isn't much fun. Some people feel grumpy, anxious or emotional, and they may not know exactly why. This is a great time to be a kind and caring friend.

Here are a few simple ways to help emotionally:
- Say kind things like, **'You've got this,'** or, **'I'm here if you need me.'**
- Be patient if they seem quiet or upset.
- Don't take it personally if they want some space.
- Offer a distraction – talk about fun stuff, play a game or watch a movie together.

Just being a **good listener** can mean so much. You don't have to solve all their problems, just show that you care.

STEP 3: HELP WITH PRACTICAL STUFF

Sometimes, it's the little things that really make a difference when someone's on their period. Some helpful things you can do are:

CARRY EXTRAS: keep a spare pad or tampon in your bag in case a friend needs one.

OFFER SUPPLIES: if someone gets their period unexpectedly, you can help by offering a pad, helping them find the bathroom, or lending them a jacket to tie around their waist if they're worried about a leak.

CHECK IN QUIETLY: ask in private, **'Are you okay?'** or, **'Do you need anything?'** so they don't feel embarrassed.

GET THEM WATER OR A SNACK: some people might feel dizzy, tired or hungry during their period. A bottle of water or a snack bar can be a big help.

LET THEM REST: if someone is feeling unwell during class, P.E. or lunch, give them space or even offer to walk with them to the nurse's office.

WARMTH HELPS: a hot water bottle or warm drink can soothe cramps. If you're at home or staying at someone else's house, see if you can get one for them.

You don't have to do everything perfectly, and certainly not everything on that list, but even one small act of kindness can make a big difference.

STEP 4: RESPECT THEIR PRIVACY

Not everyone wants to talk about their period openly and that's okay. Some people feel shy, especially if they're new to getting their period or have had a leak or accident.

HERE'S HOW TO SHOW RESPECT AND PROTECT THEIR PRIVACY:

Never shout about it or tell others without their permission – it is a private thing, but not a bad thing.

Be discreet if you're offering a pad or tampon, you can pass it quietly or put it in their bag.

If someone has a stain on their clothes, tell them **privately and kindly**, not in front of others.

Don't post or **joke** about someone's period on social media or group chats – that is never okay.

Being a respectful friend means keeping personal things private, even when you're trying to help.

STEP 5: HELP CREATE A SUPPORTIVE ENVIRONMENT

If you're in school or a shared space, there are things everyone can do to make it easier for people who have their period. **You could:**

ENCOURAGE your school to have free period products in bathrooms – and maybe have a small supply of a range of products in your own home for guests and visitors.

SUPPORT a classmate who asks for a break or to go to the nurse.

REMIND others not to joke about periods, it's not funny for the person experiencing it.

BE SOMEONE people can count on for help or advice.

If you're a boy or someone who doesn't get a period, you can still help by being **kind**, learning about how periods work, and treating people with **respect** when they're on their period (and at any other time, too!).

HELPFUL THINGS TO SAY:

DO YOU WANT TO TALK?

I HAVE A PAD IF YOU NEED ONE.

YOU'RE DOING GREAT.

IT'S OKAY TO REST.

THINGS *NOT* TO SAY:

EW GROSS!

JUST GET OVER IT.

ARE YOU ON YOUR PERIOD OR SOMETHING?

YOU'RE ACTING WEIRD.

STOP BEING SO EMOTIONAL.

EVERYONE DESERVES SUPPORT

Being there for someone on their period is about being kind, respectful and helpful. It's not just about giving out pads or helping in emergencies, it's about making sure people feel safe, seen and supported.

Here's the thing: everyone needs help sometimes. And when you support someone else, they're more likely to support you back when you need it, whether that's during your own period, a hard day at school, or anything else. Caring for someone on their period just takes empathy, awareness and kindness. If you can do those things, you're already a wonderful friend, sibling or classmate.

Empathy

Awareness

Kindness

PERIODS AROUND THE WORLD

Did you know that on any given day, around **800 million people** are menstruating? Yep, it's totally natural, but how people *think* and *talk* about periods depends a lot on where they live, what they believe, and what they've been taught.

In some places, getting your first period is a **big celebration**. In others, it can be more difficult to talk about or even seen in a negative light. But understanding how different cultures view menstruation helps us break stereotypes, fight stigma and support everyone who menstruates, **no matter where they're from**.

PERIODS AROUND THE WORLD: THE GOOD, THE DIFFERENT AND THE WOW

Some cultures treat a first period like a coming-of-age celebration, kind of like a birthday mixed with a graduation.

HERE ARE A FEW EXAMPLES:

INDIA: in parts of South India, girls are celebrated with a family gathering called *Ritu Kala Samskara*. Girls receive new clothes, gifts and blessings.

INDIGENOUS AMERICAN TRIBES: some tribes, such as the Navajo and Apache, hold ceremonies to honour the connection between a girl, nature and womanhood.

FIJI: some Fijian communities have rituals involving special mats and feasts to mark a girl's first period and educate her about its significance.

PERIOD MYTHS

Unfortunately, not all beliefs about periods are kind or true. In many places, periods are wrapped in silence and prejudice. These negative opinions can make people feel embarrassed about their periods, stop girls from doing everyday things, and even lead to unfair treatment. For example, in some **cultural traditions**, women who are having their period do not visit temples or go to places of worship, based on traditional beliefs that menstruation was associated with uncleanliness. Although the concerns about uncleanliness may have reduced, the custom that women should not go to religious places during their period still stands in some cultures.

WHAT IS PERIOD POVERTY?

Imagine missing school because you don't have a pad. Or feeling ashamed because no one ever explained periods to you. That's period poverty. It means not having access to pads, tampons or other sanitary products, clean water and toilets, or accurate information and support from family, school or your community.

SOME FACTS:
- In **Sub-Saharan Africa**, 1 in 10 girls may skip school during their period.
- In **India**, many girls drop out of school after puberty.
- In the **UK**, nearly 1 in 5 girls struggle to afford or access period products.

PEOPLE ARE FIGHTING BACK AND YOU CAN TOO!

All over the world, young people, educators, and activists are working to get rid of period shame and make life better for menstruating people.

HERE'S HOW:

- **Schools** are adding period education to the curriculum.
- **Social media** campaigns like *#PeriodPositive* are spreading awareness.
- **Movies** like *Pad Man* are bringing attention to period health.
- **Governments** (like in New Zealand and Scotland) are giving out free pads in schools and public places.

HOW YOU CAN HELP BREAK THE STIGMA

Whether you have periods or not, you can be part of the movement. Here's what you can do:

1 **Talk about it.** Don't whisper the word 'period'. Say it and normalize it.

2 **Share products.** Give period products to your friends or classmates if they need one, or donate pads to or support period charities.

3 **Learn the facts.** Bust the myths when you hear them.

4 **Include everyone.** Boys and non-menstruating people need period education too.

5 **Celebrate it.** Periods are a sign of health and strength, not something to hide.

Periods shouldn't be treated like a secret or a curse. **They're a part of life**, a part of health, and a part of what makes human beings *human*. But not everyone feels comfortable talking about them, especially if they come from a background where periods are seen as something shameful or off-limits. That's why **kindness**, **openness** and **understanding** matter so much.

Every time we speak up, share **knowledge** or show **support**, we help create a world where people aren't afraid or embarrassed about something so **normal**. Let's ditch the stigma and build a future where everyone is treated with **dignity**.

TALKING ABOUT PERIODS: COMMUNICATION AND SUPPORT

Periods are a **natural part of life**, yet many people still feel awkward or embarrassed talking about them. Whether it's bringing up the topic with your parents, chatting with friends or handling a tricky moment at school, knowing how to talk about your period can make life easier and help break down the **stigma** that often surrounds menstruation.

Periods are a personal thing, but they are not an embarrassment or something that can't be spoken out. Half the humans living on the planet have a period between the ages of about 15 and 50, and until relatively recently they were something that was an embarrassing secret – **that is changing!**

So, let's explore how to navigate period conversations with **confidence**: at home, with friends and in social settings, and how to ask for help when you need it.

Your home should be a **safe space** to talk about your body and health. But sometimes it's common to feel shy about starting the conversation, especially if it's at the beginning of your period journey, or you're not sure how your family will react.

TIPS FOR TALKING TO PARENTS OR GUARDIANS:

1 **Choose a calm, private moment.** Pick a time when you won't be interrupted, like during a walk, driving home from school, at bedtime or while doing a quiet activity together.

2 **Be honest and clear.** You could say, **'I think I just started my period,'** or, **'I have some questions about periods and I'm not sure how to ask.'** Most adults will appreciate your honesty and be glad to help.

3 **Ask for what you need.** Whether it's pads, pain relief or just a listening ear, let them know. **'Can you help me get some help managing my periods?'** or, **'I would like to try these,'** or, **'My periods really hurt and I don't know what to do,'** or, **'The toilets at school are really difficult.'**

4 **If it feels easier to talk to one particular adult, start there.** That might be your mum, dad, aunt, big sister or another adult – your teacher or school nurse would also be a really good person you could talk to.

TALKING TO FRIENDS ABOUT PERIODS

Friends can be an amazing source of support and comfort, especially when they're going through the same things. Talking about periods with friends helps everyone feel less alone and more confident.

HOW TO START THE CONVERSATION:

1 **Bring it up naturally. 'Do you ever get really tired during your period?'** or, **'What kind of pads do you use?'** can be easy openers.

2 **Share your experience. 'I started my period at school today and didn't have a pad; it was so stressful.'** Personal stories invite others to share theirs.

3 **Be supportive.** If a friend mentions their period, listen without judgment. A simple, **'That's difficult, I get it,'** can be comforting – a problem shared is a problem halved.

WHAT IF SOMEONE MAKES A JOKE OR REACTS BADLY?

Sometimes people don't understand periods, or they might have normalized shame or stigma. If a friend or someone at school laughs or teases, you can say:

'IT'S A NORMAL PART OF LIFE, ACTUALLY.'

'THAT'S NOT FUNNY. I'D RATHER WE RESPECT EACH OTHER.'

You deserve friends who respect you and your body, just like you should do the same back.

NAVIGATING PERIODS AT SCHOOL

Managing your periods at school can be tricky, especially when you're not sure how to ask for what you need or when accidents happen. But with a little planning and confidence, you can handle it smoothly.

WHAT TO KEEP IN YOUR SCHOOL BAG:
- A few **pads** or **tampons** in a **small pouch**, or a spare pair of **period pants**.
- An **extra pair of pants** in case of any leaks.
- **Pain relief**, such as ibuprofen or paracetamol (if allowed by your school).
- A **small plastic bag** for wrapping up used products.

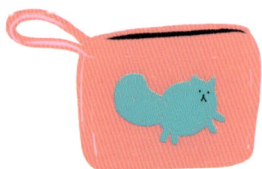

Remember, if you forget all of these things, you can always fold some tissue paper in the bathroom and put it like an emergency pad in your underwear until you can get hold of a pad or tampon.

IF YOU NEED TO ASK A TEACHER OR SCHOOL NURSE; IT'S OKAY TO QUIETLY SAY:

'I NEED TO GO TO THE NURSE.'

'I NEED TO USE THE BATHROOM URGENTLY.'

Most teachers understand that students need privacy. Some schools have free period products in the nurse's office or bathrooms. If you're not sure, ask a staff member you trust.

IF YOU LEAK OR HAVE AN ACCIDENT:
First of all, it happens to **everyone** at some point. If you leak:

1 Tie a sweatshirt or jacket around your waist.

2 Ask to go to the nurse or office to change.

3 **Don't panic**, most people won't notice, and if they do, they'll likely understand.

TALKING ABOUT PERIODS IN SOCIAL SETTINGS

What if you're hanging out with friends, at a sleepover or on a trip, and your period starts?

AT SLEEPOVERS OR SCHOOL CAMPS/TRIPS:
Remember to bring your supplies and a small bag for disposal. Let a friend or adult know privately if you need help, if you are really struggling you can always ask to ring home for more support. And if someone makes a rude comment, speak up or walk away.

IN PUBLIC PLACES:
When you are out and about, carry a few supplies in your bag, just in case. If you need to ask a friend or staff for help, it's okay. You don't have to announce it to everyone. Just do what makes you feel most comfortable. There's no shame in asking. Remember the folded tissue paper as a last resort until you can get hold of some sanitary products!

BUILDING A PERIOD-POSITIVE COMMUNITY

By talking openly and kindly about periods you're helping break taboos and create a more supportive world for everyone else who has a period.

You can support a friend going through her first period,

share period resources or information with classmates, encourage your school to stock free period products, or talk to boys and friends about periods in a respectful way, because the more people who understand, the better.

CONFIDENCE COMES WITH PRACTICE

Talking about your period might feel awkward at first and that's totally okay. It takes practice to get comfortable, just like with anything new. But the more you speak up, the easier it gets. By opening up, you're not only taking care of yourself, you're also helping others feel seen and heard.

NUTRITION AND EXERCISE: SUPPORTING YOUR CYCLE

Your period is a time when your body goes through natural but complex hormonal changes. While it might sometimes feel uncomfortable or tiring, taking care of yourself through healthy food choices, good hydration and gentle movement can make a big difference.

Let's explore how you can feel better and stay strong throughout your menstrual cycle.

FOODS THAT CAN HELP DURING YOUR PERIOD

Food plays an important role in how you feel during your period. Some foods can help **ease cramps**, **reduce bloating**, **boost your mood** and even improve your **energy levels**. Others may make symptoms worse. Eating well-balanced meals can support your body's natural needs during your entire cycle.

1 Iron-rich foods

When you have your period, you lose a small amount of blood, and with it, some iron. Low iron levels can lead to fatigue or dizziness, and if you have heavy periods you can be more at risk. But even if your periods aren't particularly heavy, it is still a good idea to be aware of the things you eat that can boost your iron levels.

FOR EXAMPLE:
- Lean red meat (beef, lamb, pork)
- Leafy green vegetables like spinach and broccoli
- Dried fruit, nuts and beans
- Fortified breakfast cereals – many cereals are fortified which means they have extra vitamins and minerals added, and can be a healthy source of iron and vitamins. Have a look at the ingredients list of your favourite cereal to see if it has been fortified!

TOP TIP: eating iron-rich foods alongside foods that contain vitamin C (like oranges, tomatoes or peppers) helps your body to absorb the iron better.

2 Magnesium and potassium for cramp relief
It's thought that these minerals may help relax muscles and ease cramping.

GREAT OPTIONS INCLUDE:
- Bananas
- Avocados
- Nuts and seeds (such as almonds and pumpkin seeds)
- Spinach or leafy greens

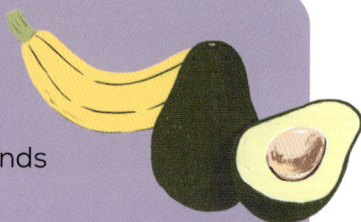

3 Omega-3 fatty acids for inflammation
Omega-3s may help to reduce period pain as they have anti-inflammatory properties. They are found in fatty fish oils and some seeds and nuts.

TRY EATING:
- Salmon, mackerel or sardines – try to have at least one portion of oily fish each week as it is the best source of omega 3
- Flaxseeds or chia seeds
- Walnuts

4 **Calcium and vitamin D**

These nutrients support your bones and may help reduce PMS symptoms. They are mainly found in milk and dairy.

GOOD OPTIONS ARE:
- Yogurt, milk or cheese
  (or fortified plant-based alternatives)
- Eggs
- Fortified non-dairy milks (such as almond or soy milk)

FOODS TO LIMIT OR AVOID

While some cravings are normal, certain foods can actually make your period symptoms worse. Good healthy eating is important throughout your teenage years, and life, so here are a few things to try and avoid having too much of:

- **Salty snacks** → can increase bloating and water retention. Remember there is often salt hidden in foods, so try to avoid adding extra.
- **Caffeine** → affects your sleep which can make you feel tired.
- **Sugary foods** → can cause energy crashes and make you feel sluggish.
- **Greasy or fried foods** → may irritate your digestive system and cause discomfort.

Balance is key. You don't need to be perfect, just aim to support your body rather than work against it.

HYDRATION: WHY WATER MATTERS EVEN MORE DURING YOUR PERIOD

Drinking enough water is always important, but during your period, it's essential.

HERE'S WHY STAYING HYDRATED HELPS:

- **Reduces bloating:** drinking more water helps your body flush toxins and fluids through. Bloating is often due to gases, not water!
- **Eases cramps:** dehydration can make cramps worse. Muscles (including your uterus) need water to function properly.
- **Improves energy:** fatigue during your period can be made worse by dehydration.
- **Helps digestion:** water supports smoother bowel movements, which can be helpful when hormones slow down digestion.
- **Reduces headaches:** having a good fluid intake supports your blood pressure and reduces headaches.

Tips for staying hydrated:

- Carry a reusable water bottle and take sips regularly.
- Add fruit like cucumber to make water taste more interesting.

- Eat hydrating foods such as watermelon, cucumber, oranges or soup.

HOW MUCH WATER?

Aim for at least 6–8 glasses (about 1.5–2 litres) a day – more if you're active or it's hot outside. Why not try measuring out 2 litres of water in a bottle and see if you can drink the whole thing over a full day? You can even buy some reusable water bottles that have times marked out on them, to give you a guide for how much to drink each day and how regularly.

SAFE EXERCISE DURING YOUR PERIOD: MOVE TO FEEL BETTER

It's a myth that you shouldn't exercise during your period. In fact, light to moderate movement can relieve cramps, boost your mood and improve circulation. The key is to listen to your body and choose the right kind of activity.

BENEFITS OF EXERCISING ON YOUR PERIOD:
- **Reduces cramps:** exercise releases natural painkillers (endorphins) that help reduce pain.
- **Boosts mood:** movement combats anxiety or irritability by increasing feel-good hormones.

- **Improves energy:** light cardio exercises can help you feel less sluggish.
- **Supports sleep:** gentle exercise can improve the quality of your rest, which may be affected by hormones.

TYPES OF SAFE AND GENTLE EXERCISES

You don't need to run a marathon! These activities can be helpful during menstruation – and in fact at any time during your cycle. There is lots of evidence showing that physical exercise is good for your body and your mind any day and every day you do it!

Walking

Even a short 15- or 30-minute walk can increase blood flow to your muscles and reduce cramps in your tummy. Getting outside is also great for you for all sorts of reasons – period or not!

Yoga

Certain yoga poses are specifically good for easing cramps, back pain and tension. Try child's pose, cat-cow stretch, or legs resting up against the wall.

Stretching

Gentle stretching can relieve bloating and help with flexibility. Even if you can't manage a full-on yoga session, some lovely stretching can do you the world of good.

Swimming

Swimming can be very soothing when you are having your period. The water pressure may temporarily reduce flow and ease cramps. In the past, swimming during your period was always viewed as a difficult thing unless you were using a tampon or a menstrual cup. More recent evidence has shown that the pressure of the water actually reduces blood flow, so unless your period is very heavy you can safely swim without using any period products at all – you won't leave a trail of blood behind you, and you won't cause any hygiene issues as it is most likely that you won't lose a significant amount of blood in the pool. However, remember the flow will resume once you leave the water, so you might want to have your preferred method on standby! There are also period-friendly swimming costumes (a bit like period pants) that can be used during your period, as long as your flow isn't incredibly heavy. Sanitary pads cannot be used when you are swimming because they will absorb pool water, but tampons or menstrual cups are fine.

Low-impact cardio

Try cycling, walking or dancing, just keep it at a comfortable pace.

WHEN TO TAKE IT EASY

Everyone's body is different. Some people feel energized during their period, while others feel tired, achy or emotional. It's okay to rest at any time, but especially if you have severe cramps or heavy bleeding, you feel dizzy or weak, or you're extra fatigued. Listen to your body and give yourself permission to slow down.

TAKEAWAY MESSAGE: BALANCE, NOURISHMENT AND LISTENING TO YOUR BODY

Taking care of yourself during your period isn't just about **'getting through it'**, it's about helping your body and mind feel their best. When you eat nourishing, balanced meals, stay well hydrated and move gently and safely, you'll likely notice improvements in your cramps, energy, mood and overall comfort.

WHEN THINGS AREN'T NORMAL: KNOWING WHEN TO SEEK HELP

Starting your periods is a **normal part of growing up**, and for many teenagers, periods can take some time to settle into a regular pattern. However, sometimes problems with your periods can be a sign that something more serious is going on. While many changes in periods are completely normal during the teenage years, it's important to understand when irregular or unusual periods might be a symptom of a gynaecological problem (gynaecological just means anything to do with your reproductive system – basically anything you see in the diagram on page 11!). Knowing what to look out for can help you get the right support and care. Even the most common problems are quite rare, but it is worth having an understanding about the sorts of problems that can happen.

WHAT IS AN 'ABNORMAL' PERIOD?

First, let's understand what **'normal'** means. A typical cycle is around 21 to 35 days long, and a period can last anywhere from 3 to 7 days. However, for the first few years after your periods begin, it is common for cycles to be irregular.

Periods are considered abnormal if:
- They are extremely heavy (soaking through pads/tampons every couple of hours)
- They last more than 7 days
- They happen more than every 21 days or less often than every 35 days
- You don't have a period for more than 3 months (after periods have become established and regular)
- They come with significant pain or other worrying symptoms

Let's explore some of the conditions that might cause these signs.

POLYCYSTIC OVARY SYNDROME (PCOS)

WHAT IS IT?
Polycystic Ovary Syndrome **(PCOS)** is one of the most common hormone-related conditions in teenage girls. It affects how the ovaries work and can lead to irregular periods, among other symptoms.

Common signs include:
- Irregular or missed periods
- Excess hair growth on the face or body
- Acne that doesn't improve with standard treatment
- Weight gain or difficulty losing weight

WHY DOES IT HAPPEN?

PCOS is caused by a **hormone imbalance**. The ovaries produce too much of certain hormones (mainly testosterone), which can stop ovulation (the release of an egg), leading to missed or irregular periods. It is the elevated testosterone and male hormones that causes the symptoms of acne and excess body hair.

WHAT CAN BE DONE?

PCOS can't be 'cured', but it can be managed with lifestyle changes, hormonal medicines and support from a doctor. The most important way of reducing any longer term health risks of PCOS is by keeping a healthy weight through exercise and healthy eating. If you have concerns about irregular periods, periods that have stopped for 6 months once your periods have become established, then you should arrange to see your GP.

STOPPED PERIODS

If you have had regular periods for a year or more and then they stop – typically for 3–6 months, you should arrange to see your GP. There are many reasons why periods might stop, most commonly due to low body weight, stress, poor nutrition or excessive exercise.

WHAT CAN BE DONE?

Recovery usually involves reducing stress, gaining weight and cutting back on intense exercise. It is usually body weight and nutrition that need to be addressed and then the periods will fall into place.

ENDOMETRIOSIS

WHAT IS IT?

Endometriosis is a condition where tissue similar to the lining of the uterus grows in other areas, such as on the ovaries, fallopian tubes or other parts of the body. This can cause very painful periods, because just as the lining of the uterus enlarges and thickens and then bleeds, the same can happen with the other tissues grown elsewhere in the body and this causes the pain.

Common signs include:
- Severe period pain that doesn't improve with painkillers
- Pain when going to the toilet (for a poo or a wee) during periods
- Nausea or vomiting during periods
- Fatigue and low energy

WHY DOES IT HAPPEN?

Doctors aren't exactly sure what causes endometriosis, but there are many theories including a link to hormonal and immune system issues. It can run in families (if your sister or mum is affected then your chances of developing endometriosis are increased) and often begins in the teen years. One theory is that if, during your period, some blood flows backwards through the fallopian tubes, then this tissue can attach to other places in the pelvis and grow. Another possibility is that the immune system might play a role. These are just theories, and endometriosis is a difficult condition to diagnose (it usually needs doctors to have a look inside the abdomen with a telescopic camera) and treat.

WHAT CAN BE DONE?

While endometriosis can't be cured, it can be managed with medication, pain relief and, in more severe cases, surgery. Early diagnosis can help prevent long-term complications.

BLEEDING DISORDERS

WHAT ARE THEY?

Some people may have conditions that affect how well they form blood clots. In girls, these conditions can cause extremely heavy periods.

Common signs include:

- Very heavy periods (changing pads/tampons every couple of hours)
- Periods lasting more than 7–8 days
- Frequent nosebleeds
- Easily bruising
- Bleeding a lot after dental work or surgery

WHY DOES IT HAPPEN?

In people with bleeding disorders, the body doesn't make enough of the proteins needed for blood to clot properly. These conditions can run in families, and so you may hear about other family members who have had heavy periods, or problems with bruising.

WHAT CAN BE DONE?

Doctors can run blood tests to check for clotting issues. Treatments might include medications to help with clotting or hormonal treatments to control period flow.

THYROID DISORDERS

WHAT IS IT?

The thyroid is a small gland in the neck that controls many body processes, including metabolism (how your body turns food into energy) and menstruation. If your thyroid is either overactive or underactive it can affect your periods.

Common signs include:
- Irregular or very light periods
- Fatigue or sleep problems
- Weight changes
- Dry skin or hair loss
- Feeling cold or hot all the time

WHAT CAN BE DONE?

Blood tests can check thyroid function. Treatment usually involves medication to balance thyroid hormone levels.

WHAT CAN I DO IF MY PERIODS ARE VERY HEAVY?

THE FIRST QUESTION TO DECIDE IS WHEN IS A PERIOD TOO HEAVY?

The medical definitions are that a period is considered abnormally long if it lasts **more than 7 days** – and it is unusually heavy if you need to change a larger pad or tampon **more than every 2 hours**. Obviously, particularly when you are younger, even periods that are lighter than this can be difficult to manage. If you are finding your periods difficult to manage, speak to your mum or a parent or adult close to you and consider going to see your GP for further advice. Your GP might think about whether you need a blood test, for example to check your blood count.

The first treatments that may be suggested will likely be **non-hormone treatments** such as ibuprofen. If this is taken regularly during the first 48 hours of your period, this can reduce the amount of blood you lose by up to a third (30%). This can make a real difference to how easy things are to manage at school, for example. There are another group of medicines which prevent bleeding by helping blood clots last longer. Tranexamic acid is an example of this and can reduce blood loss by as much as 50%. You should speak to your GP if you think any of these treatments could be right and necessary for you.

Finally, your GP might consider **hormonal treatment**. You might be prescribed progesterone or the contraceptive pill, which can make your periods about 50% lighter and also more predictable. After the first month or so, you can even take some types of pill continuously to avoid having any periods at all. There is a (very low) risk of some **side effects** such as blood clots when taking these extra hormones, and they are not suitable for everyone, so it is really important to discuss the options with your GP. It's not good to start this treatment if you don't really need to, but it is an option for difficult periods once you are a little older and particularly if your periods are not otherwise manageable. These medicines work by stopping your ovaries from releasing eggs and this can reduce or prevent many of the symptoms that some people can experience.

There are some **other treatments** that can be considered – some research has suggested that calcium, vitamin B6 and magnesium supplements can all have a role in helping manage your periods and these supplements can be helpful. Always discuss the vitamin and supplement approach with your GP or pharmacist before trialling.

WHEN TO SEE A DOCTOR

It's normal to have some irregularity in your periods during the first few years, but you should talk to your GP or school nurse if:

- **You haven't started your periods by the age of 15.**
- **Your period was regular but has suddenly stopped for more than 3 months.**
- **Your periods are extremely heavy or painful.**
- **You're feeling tired, dizzy or faint during your period.**
- **You're worried about your symptoms or your body.**

It can be scary to talk about these things at first, but remember: doctors are here to help, not judge – they will see many patients with period problems every single week and your problems will not be unusual to them. The sooner you get support, the better you can manage your health.

PERIOD POSITIVITY: EMBRACING YOUR CYCLE

For many years, periods have been surrounded by silence, shame and stigma. People were taught to whisper about them, hide their period products and act like menstruation was something embarrassing. But things are changing and you are part of that change. Period positivity is a movement and a mindset that encourages everyone, especially girls and young people, to view menstruation as natural and nothing to be ashamed of.

CHANGING THE WAY WE THINK ABOUT PERIODS

A positive mindset about menstruation starts with how we talk about it. Your period is a sign that your body is healthy and working just as it should. It's not gross, dirty or something to hide. When we change how we think and talk about periods, we begin to break down the walls of embarrassment and replace them with understanding and confidence.

PERIOD POSITIVITY MEANS SAYING THINGS LIKE:

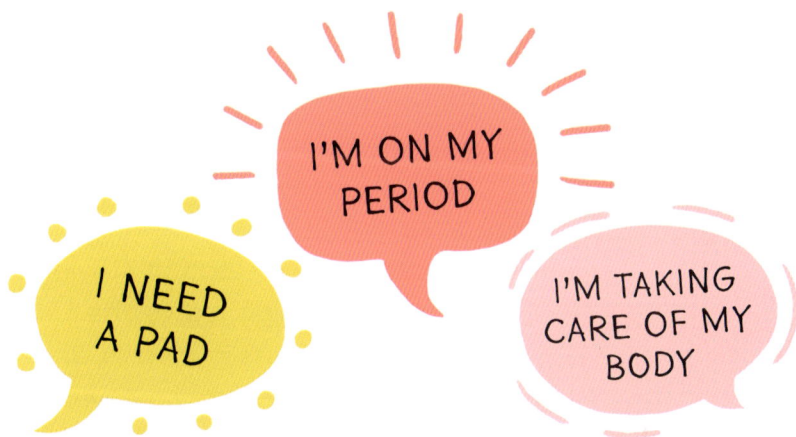

I'M ON MY PERIOD

I NEED A PAD

I'M TAKING CARE OF MY BODY

It also means understanding that there's no one 'right' way to have a period. Everyone's experience is different, some people have light periods, some have heavy ones, some feel tired, others don't. Some people notice their emotions might be up and down depending on their cycle, where others won't. What matters is knowing your body, being kind to yourself and trusting that you are doing your best.

When you adopt a positive attitude toward your period, you allow yourself to feel **empowered** rather than embarrassed. You learn to take care of yourself physically and emotionally, and you're more likely to speak up when something feels wrong.

STORIES OF STRENGTH AND OVERCOMING STIGMA

Across the globe, many people have overcome period stigma and become voices of change. These stories are proof that speaking up can inspire others and make a real difference.

Amika George is a young British activist who started the *Free Periods* campaign when she was just 17. She learned that many girls in the UK were missing school because they couldn't afford period products. Instead of staying silent, Amika took action. Her campaign led to the UK government funding free period products in schools, and she sparked a global conversation about period poverty and shame. Amika has even appeared on *The Times* Most Influential Teens list and *Teen Vogue* 21 under 21. What a superstar!

Kiran Gandhi is a musician who ran the London Marathon in 2015 while free-bleeding, meaning she chose not to wear a tampon or pad or use any other period product. She did this to raise awareness about people who can't access menstrual products and to fight the idea that periods must always be hidden. Her bold choice got people talking and challenged old ideas about what's '**appropriate**'.

In many cultures, girls have faced isolation or exclusion during their periods. But more and more girls and women are sharing their stories, calling out these practices, and helping their communities grow in understanding and kindness.

When you hear stories like these, or when you share your own, you will come to realize that periods are not a weakness. They are a sign of strength, maturity and the ability to speak up even when it's uncomfortable.

PERIOD ACTIVISM: SPEAKING UP AND MAKING CHANGE

ACTIVISM is basically taking action to make positive changes about something you really care about in society. It can start small, like telling your friends it's okay to talk about their periods, or reminding your school that bathrooms should always be stocked with products. But it can grow into something powerful.

You don't have to be on a big stage to make change. You can...

- Organize a pad or tampon donation project.
- Ask your school to include better period education.
- Share posts that celebrate period positivity online.
- Speak out about your experience and support others to do the same.

Activism means using your voice to stand up for what you believe in. If you believe that everyone deserves dignity, education and respect during their period, then you are already a period-positive activist.

YOUR ROLE IN A PERIOD-POSITIVE WORLD

You have the power to create a world where periods are treated with respect, not embarrassment, or worse ... disgust. Where young people feel proud of their bodies, and no one is left behind because they can't afford a pad, or because they're too scared to ask for help. Being period positive doesn't mean pretending every moment of your cycle is easy. It means accepting that it's okay to feel grumpy, tired or in pain, and it's also okay to take time for yourself, to rest, or to celebrate your body for all it does.

You are part of a new generation that isn't afraid to speak up. Whether you're just starting your period journey or have had it for years, you can be a voice for kindness, knowledge and change.

FINAL THOUGHTS AND ENCOURAGEMENT

In writing **Periods: Everything You Need to Know**, I wanted to not only teach you all about your period, but to help you understand your body, your cycle and yourself better.

Your period is a **normal, natural** part of growing up. It's one way your body tells you that it's becoming strong, capable and ready for the next stage in life. Every person's cycle is different, some are regular, others take time to settle. Some have cramps, others don't. There's no 'right' way to have a period. What matters is learning to listen to your body and take care of it in the way that **works best** for you.

You now know about the menstrual cycle, the role of hormones, and the amazing way your body prepares for a period each month. You've discovered the different types of menstrual products you can choose from, whether it's pads, tampons, cups or period pants, and how to manage your periods with confidence. You've also learned that it's okay to talk about periods openly. They're not gross, shameful or weird. They're a sign of health, growth and power.

As you move forward, remember: having a period doesn't limit you. You can still play sports, go to school, laugh with friends and chase your dreams. Your period is just one part of you – it doesn't define you. What does define you is your strength, kindness, courage and how you show up for yourself and others.

So, take pride in this journey. Whether you've had your first period already or you're still waiting, or even if you've been having them for a while already, know that you are not alone. Millions of people around the world are walking this same path, and each of them is figuring it out, just like you.

YOU'VE GOT THIS. PERIOD.

GLOSSARY

Activism
Taking action to make positive changes about something you care about.

Amenorrhea
When a person doesn't get their period for a long time (usually three months or more). This can happen for different reasons, like stress, extreme exercise or certain health conditions.

Cervix
The lower part of the uterus (womb) that opens into the vagina. During your period, menstrual blood flows from the uterus through the cervix and vagina, and out of the body.

Cramps
Aching or throbbing pain in the lower belly or back that can happen before or during a period. They're caused by the uterus tightening.

Cycle (menstrual cycle)
The monthly process your body goes through to get ready for a possible pregnancy. It includes your period and the days in between. A full cycle is usually around 28 days, but it can be longer or shorter.

Discharge
A normal fluid that comes out of the vagina. It helps keep the vagina clean and healthy. Discharge can change during the menstrual cycle.

Egg (ovum)
A tiny cell produced by the ovaries. Each month, one egg is released during ovulation. If the egg isn't fertilized, it's part of what leaves the body during a period.

Endometrium
The lining of the uterus. It thickens to get ready for a possible pregnancy. If pregnancy doesn't happen, this lining leaves the body through the vagina – that's what your period is.

Fallopian tubes
Two thin tubes that connect the ovaries to the uterus. This is where the egg travels after being released from the ovary.

GP
This is short for General Practitioner and just means your doctor.

Hormones
Chemical messengers in your body that help control lots of things – like growth, sleep and the menstrual cycle. Hormones can also play a role in your moods and emotions.

Menarche
The first period a girl ever gets. It's a sign that puberty is underway and the reproductive system is starting to work.

Menorrhagia
Very heavy periods that need pad or tampon changes every couple of hours.

Menstrual products
Things used to catch or absorb period blood. These include pads, tampons, menstrual cups and period pants.

Menstruation
Another word for having your period – when blood comes out of the vagina as the body sheds the lining of the uterus.

Oestrogen
One of the main hormones that control the menstrual cycle. It kick starts puberty and helps get the body ready for ovulation.

Ovaries
Two small organs on either side of the uterus. They store all the eggs you will need during your life, and make hormones like oestrogen and progesterone.

Ovulation
When an ovary releases an egg – usually around the middle of the menstrual cycle.

PMS (premenstrual syndrome)
Feelings or symptoms some people get in the days before their period – like mood swings, sore breasts, headaches or bloating.

Period
The days when you bleed from the vagina as part of your monthly cycle. It usually lasts between three to seven days.

Period poverty
Not having access to pads, tampons or other sanitary products, clean water and toilets or accurate information and support from family, school or your community.

Progesterone
Another important hormone in the menstrual cycle. It helps prepare the body for pregnancy after ovulation.

Puberty

The time when your body starts to change and develop into an adult. It includes getting your period, growing breasts, body hair and more.

Spotting

Very light bleeding that can happen between periods. It's usually just a few drops and can happen for many reasons.

Tampon

A soft wad of cotton that is placed inside the vagina to absorb period blood. Some have applicators to help insert them.

Uterus (womb)

An organ in the lower belly where a baby can grow during pregnancy. It sheds its lining during a period if there's no pregnancy.

Vagina

The part of the body that connects the uterus to the outside. It's where menstrual blood comes out, and it's also called the birth canal.

INDEX